THE SPIRIT OF NEBRASKA

A HISTORY OF HUSKER GAME DAY TRADITIONS
THE TUNNEL WALK, MASCOTS, CHEER, & MORE

DEBRA KLEVE WHITE   FOREWORD BY TOM OSBORNE

THE SPIRIT OF NEBRASKA

A HISTORY OF HUSKER GAME DAY TRADITIONS
THE TUNNEL WALK, MASCOTS, CHEER, & MORE

LINCOLN, NEBRASKA

The Spirit of Nebraska: A History of Husker Game Day Traditions — the Tunnel Walk, Mascots, Cheer, and More

©2019 Debra Kleve White. All Rights Reserved. No part of this book may be reproduced in any form without written permission from the publisher.

Published by Cheerful Books LLC. Photos and stories have been reproduced with the permission of the respective copyright holders, and are cited directly with the references made, or in the Photo Credits section located at the back of this volume.

For contact information, visit www.SpiritOfNebraska.com.

The author has put forth a best effort toward accuracy to create a historically correct timeline and history. Due to a lack of some recorded history, and the fact that squad members can change during the school year, there may be unintended errors. It is impossible when piecing together the past to account for all information; however, the best, reasonable effort has been put forth.

Paperback, black/white: 978-0-9980388-1-0
Hardcover, color insert: 978-0-9980388-2-7
Hardcover, full color: 978-0-9980388-6-5
Mobi: 978-0-9980388-3-4
EPUB: 978-0-9980388-4-1
Audiobook: 978-0-9980388-5-8

Cataloging-in-Publication Data on file with the publisher.
Library of Congress Control Number: 2018964351

Publishing and Production by Concierge Marketing Inc.

Printed and bound in the United States of America
10 9 8 7 6 5 4 3 2 1

In memory of my mother, a Husker fan. With love and admiration to my family: my husband, Greg; my sons, Ryan Gregory and Nathan James; my daughters-in-law, Keri and Kristen; my grandchildren, Houston James, Honor Leigh, Molly Elizabeth, Hayes Ryan, Cameron Watson, and Collin Gregory.

To lead by example and to show that anything is possible, and dreams do come true. Dream on.

Contents

Foreword	IX
Introduction	1
1. The Greatest Fans in College Football	5
2. Sis-Boom-Ahh – Yell Squad Skyrockets to Popularity	15
3. The Beginning of Nebraska Football, School Spirit, and the Ushering in of Cheerleading	49
4. The Ever-Lasting Influence of Roscoe and Louise Pound	69
5. The Secrets of the Innocents Society	97
6. How the Sea of Red Was Almost a Sea of Old Gold	103
7. "No Place Like Nebraska" – University Yells and Songs	105
Photo Album	[A] 133
8. Of Corn Cobs and Tassels – Student Pep Organizations Drive School Spirit	149
9. Pride of the Cornhusker State – The Band	169
10. The Razzle-Dazzle of the Pompon Squads and the Scarlets Dance Team	177
11. From Bugeaters to Cornhuskers and Corn Cob Man to Herbie Husker – The Lore Behind the Team Names and Mascots	185
A Final Hurrah	197
Notes, Sources, and Bibliography	199
Acknowledgments	201
About the Author	205
Photo Credits	207

FOREWORD
BY TOM OSBORNE

AS A FOOTBALL COACH FOR THIRTY-SIX YEARS AT THE UNIVERSITY OF NEBRASKA, my attention was always directed toward the playing field on game days. I was largely unaware of what was going on off the field; therefore, I must plead a fairly high level of ignorance regarding what cheerleaders, band members, and even the fans were doing on those autumn afternoons.

When Debra White asked me to write a foreword to her book concerning Husker cheer and tradition, I must confess to a certain degree of uncertainty as to what I could offer. Having said that, I was, and am, keenly aware that the culture of Husker athletics has a certain unique quality that is seldom found anywhere else in college athletics and thought that maybe I could connect that unique culture to many of the traditions and historical occurrences which Deb points out.

College football is extremely important to most of the citizens of Nebraska. I have often been curious about where this fascination with the game came from. I suppose that there are a number of reasons that one might mention: Nebraska has only one major college football team in the entire state, so there are few divided loyalties; Nebraska had a tradition of winning going back into the 1920s and '30s, which was rekindled with the arrival of Bob Devaney in 1962 and has continued with Nebraska winning more football games than any other Division One team since Bob's time; and maybe most of all, football seems to connect with a work ethic, a willingness to endure hardship, and an ability to persevere through the Dust Bowl, the Great Depression, and the rigors of frontier life.

As Vince Lombardi once said, "Football is a Spartan game," and I think that this quality seems to appeal to Nebraskans.

I was interested to learn that the game of football was first brought to the University of Nebraska by a faculty member named Frothingham, who had first observed the game while at Harvard in the 1880s. The game caught on, with Nebraska playing its first game against the Omaha YMCA in 1890. George Flippin was an outstanding player on those early Nebraska teams and was among only a handful of African American players playing the game at that time. George was elected captain and later became a doctor and practiced medicine in Nebraska for many years.

Recently there has been a good deal of media coverage about football being a violent sport. However, this perception pales in comparison to the way the game was played in those early days. President Teddy Roosevelt convened a gathering in the early 1900s to consider abolishing the game due to the large number of injuries and deaths that were occurring. The game survived that meeting and is more popular than ever today.

In addition to the groundbreaking efforts of George Flippin, Debra chronicles the efforts of Roscoe Pound to organize cheering sections and promote school spirit at Nebraska games in the 1890s. He even led a cheer in Latin, and one wonders how this would go over at today's games. Roscoe later achieved recognition in the legal field, serving as dean of the law college at Nebraska and later at Harvard.

His sister Louise was an outstanding athlete, excelling at multiple sports in an era when women competing in athletics was very rare. She also played a role in organizing women's cheering sections for athletic events and was apparently a football fan when women were seldom in attendance at football games.

Debra White was a cheerleader at Nebraska during the 1970s—my first years as a head coach. Bob Devaney's teams had won National Championships in 1970 and 1971, so my first teams were measured against a very high standard, and I am sure that I needed all the help I got from cheerleaders, fans, and the press. Since we were unsuccessful in winning National Championships and usually lost to Oklahoma during Debra's time as a cheerleader, I was somewhat surprised that she would reach out to me and request that I write a foreword to her book.

One aspect of Nebraska athletics that has endured, win or lose, has been the extraordinary sportsmanship displayed by our fans. Until reading the book, I assumed that the willingness of our fans to treat opposing teams with respect, to cheer them as they left the field, to treat opposing fans well, was something that had developed over the last thirty to forty years. I was surprised to learn that this tradition dated back as far as 1913 when students voted to cheer for the opposing team when they left the field and to applaud an opposing player when he came off the field after being injured. Students also had pep rallies for opposing teams when they came to Lincoln, so obviously this tradition of treating opponents well had roots long ago when football was first gaining a following in Nebraska.

When I think of that which sets Nebraska apart, the overall kindness of Nebraskans toward others, especially those who represent other teams and who come from other states, is probably the most noteworthy feature.

A few years ago I unexpectedly became athletic director at the University of Nebraska. During that time I had to think more broadly about the total athletic program, not just football, and part of that expanded focus involved the role that cheerleaders play. I had been somewhat aware of the hard work and discipline that went into cheerleading, but it wasn't until that time that I became fully aware of the demands put upon cheerleaders and the precision, timing, and long practice hours they bring to the table.

This book will provide valuable insights into that segment of athletics and will open the eyes of the reader to the demands of cheerleading and the role it plays in the pageantry and appeal of college athletics.

Tom Osborne, Ph. D.
Former Head Coach and Athletic Director
University of Nebraska — Lincoln

INTRODUCTION

Game day Saturday. There's nothing like it. In fall of 1977, I stepped onto the turf of Memorial Stadium in Lincoln for the first time at football pregame—wearing the coveted red-and-white-striped sweater. I was overwhelmed by the Sea of Red viewed from ground level and over more than 80,000 fans surrounding me who had come together to create, in that massive stadium steeped in tradition, the third largest city in the state of Nebraska to worship their beloved football team. I was a new member of the Yell Squad, and I was living my dream.

The fans blanketing the stadium in red, the band playing rousing school songs, and the sound of it all caroming off the stadium walls in every direction, the clapping and cheering fans on their feet—all the sights and sounds vibrated through my body and stirred up the spirit inside Memorial Stadium.

We Yell Squad members stood at the entrance of what was to become the traditional Tunnel Walk with the school mascot, Herbie Husker, leading the fans in cheers while awaiting the arrival of our coaches and team. When the fans first spotted the team running through the tunnel onto the field after touching the horseshoe mounted over their heads, the crowd unleashed an enormous roar, and we took off running too for what felt like our lives.

The team was pumped up and running out at full speed. The four cheer guys yelled at the eight of us female cheerleaders to run harder. And run we did—100 yards to the opposite end of the field's goal line in slippery-soled saddle shoes with our arms shaking huge pompons as we reached for the sky. Exhilarating—although running full speed in saddle shoes with your arms in the air is not as easy as we made it look.

Once we reached the opposing goal line, the band cranked up "No Place Like Nebraska," and we performed our kicks and twirls to the now-familiar school song. That first time was unnerving, not only because it was my initiation into being engulfed in the Sea of Red and the hoopla surrounding every game's opening festivities, but because nothing had prepared me for the sound bouncing off the stands, mingling with the fans' astounding clapping and the band's tummy-rumbling drums and horns in a cacophony of sound vibrating in every direction.

With no accurate compass for the true beat of the music, we cheerleaders were all off. Our captain yelled out, "Get it together!" After the final line of the song, "For dear old Nebraska U," we ran off to the sidelines chanting "Go Big Red," then stood at attention for the national anthem. And it was time for kickoff.

During those days we would cheer closer to the field and were spread out all along the east side student sections where we felt like part of the action. So much so we had to be careful to move out of the way of a tackle or catch that came barreling to the sidelines. Today, the NCAA restricts standing that close to the sidelines. We had a fantastic and unique experience, different from today's squads, since we were both the cheer and dance squad, heavily involved in the fan experience with megaphones and a loud speaker, close to the field, and as students, we were completely in charge of creating our stunts, dances, and fan entertainment.

As a native Nebraskan, I grew up in the heartland of America, but not as a Cornhusker faithful. Even though I was raised in Nebraska where game day Saturdays are sacred, almost holidays, I didn't have ties to the University, nor was I ever exposed to the pageantry of the game day experience.

It wasn't until I turned eighteen, graduated from high school in Seward, and moved the twenty-five miles to Lincoln in 1973 that I witnessed my first Nebraska football game. It was an experience that immediately transformed me, and I felt the school spirit deep inside with every beat of the drums and every shake of the cheerleaders' pompons. I was mesmerized by the precision and style of the cheerleaders and their contribution to game day. The game cemented my decision to find a way to attend the University of Nebraska and try out for the cheerleading squad. I could not afford to go to college, so when I first moved to Lincoln, I worked and saved my money for two years to finally enroll at the University of Nebraska.

Fast-forward a few decades to 2002. I walked into an antique store in Lincoln, Nebraska. I spotted a 1930s Cornhusker yearbook and felt a curiosity about what the cheerleading squad may have looked like during that time, so many years ago. Upon opening the yearbook, I was startled to see, staring back at me on the page, a picture of an all-male cheerleading squad. An all-male squad! I wondered how I could be affiliated with an organization that was so special to me, have a love of history, and not have any idea of the history of the cheerleading squad. This glance started the wheels in motion. This moment created a revelation. Now is the time to give back to the University of Nebraska and the Yell Squad.

My curiosity started as a little research project to find and list the names of all the cheerleaders who had cheered at the University of Nebraska. Although I began this project from scratch, I soon discovered a treasure trove of information buried at Love Library on the campus of the University, and I realized my task would entail much digging and peeling back one layer at a time to uncover the rich past.

The first discovery was that a secret group called the Innocents Society had started the Yell Squad. In fact, one of the primary reasons the University faculty gave for creating the Innocents Society was to organize cheerleading and school spirit on campus. An Innocents folder on file at Love Library contained a ledger with their old meeting minutes. The minutes that I read starting September 1903 indicated they organized the cheerleaders and selected two of their own to lead cheers. This was the official beginning of Yell Squad.

When I read the ledger, time seemed to stand still. I wondered if anyone else knew all this information. And I realized that fourteen months from the date of my discovery in the old ledger would mark a century of cheer at the University of Nebraska. I felt an enormous amount of responsibility to take immediate action. Thus, the work began for me to envision, research, and organize "100 Years of Cheer"—a celebration, reunion, and football game half-time show.

Once the mission began, one inspiring moment led to the next to keep me moving forward. The most memorable moments were conversations with former cheerleaders and the stories they told. We were complete strangers with a common bond. During conversations with former Yell Squad members, I was often asked the same question over and over again—"What made you want to organize a reunion?"

The answer to that question is obvious to me. There is absolutely nothing like being in Memorial Stadium on a football Saturday afternoon. It is often said that Nebraska fans are some of the best fans in college sports. They have connected to their football team, and that pride is felt in Memorial Stadium. There is a long-standing tradition of loyalty and school spirit, which is still very much alive in Nebraska.

It is not just football, not just the fans, not just the band, not just the Yell Squad, it is the combined pageantry with the sport that works to create these memorable moments in Memorial Stadium. Every piece plays a role in creating what every Cornhusker knows is the "Spirit of Nebraska."

This book reveals how the spirit of Nebraska was born, how the best fans in college sports evolved, how school spirit originated, the history and role of the Spirit Squad (which includes the Yell Squad/cheerleaders, the dancers known as the Scarlets, and the mascots), the significance of the color of red in the stadium, and much more.

The reunion celebrated a milestone in University of Nebraska history and tradition—over 100 years of sharing common bonds of friendship, loyalty, leadership, excellence, and dedication among the Spirit Squad family. And this book commemorates that enduring spirit.

As with anything of importance, my hope is that the University of Nebraska Spirit Squad will live on, although it is inevitable that, as history has shown, times will change, and the Spirit Squad will change with it. There is value in preserving history and celebrating the tradition of the organization—the human connection—and supporting University athletic events. May the spirit of Nebraska continue to grow.

The journey of researching for the reunion unfolded into an incredible history of people, passion, commitment, and tradition at the University of Nebraska. I am proud to use this book as an opportunity to share this story with others. "Go Big Red"—oh, and there is a story behind that too!

Debra Kleve "Klever" White
University of Nebraska Yell Squad, 1977–1980

I

THE GREATEST FANS IN COLLEGE FOOTBALL

"Through these gates pass the greatest fans in college football."

This engraved inscription proclaimed in stone above an entrance to Memorial Stadium serves as a constant reminder to the fans of their legacy and responsibility each time they pass through the stadium gates. Although they don't need reminding, the Nebraska sports fans are recognized today as some of the best fans in college football.

This sentiment is shared in the sports world and was expressed by former longtime football coach and American sports broadcaster for ESPN, Lee Corso: "I think Nebraska fans are the greatest fans in all of college football. The enthusiasm here is as good as any place, but the integrity here of the fans is the best in America. They have a respect for the game, not only for the Nebraska team, but for the opponents. The best place I've ever been is right here."

This book is a tribute to the Cornhusker fans, because loyal fans have created and continued a history that brings us to the current pageantry of the game day experience. A book on history typically starts in the beginning; however, it seems fitting to begin with the Cornhusker fans, since they fill the stadium in the fall and support the game and traditions surrounding the Husker Nation.

WHEN TO CHEER (EVEN FOR THE OTHER TEAM)

This reputation did not happen by accident. From the beginning, University of Nebraska professors set a high standard for the students in regard to manners, behavior, and respect for the opposing team. Prior to athletic competitions, University oratorical contests were popular. In the spring of 1890, the University of Nebraska was to host an interstate oratorical contest. The University considered their opponents their guests and wanted to entertain and treat them properly. The University wanted the students to understand that the reputation of the University was at stake. *The Hesperian* newspaper reported the University's message to the students:

> *We cannot afford to allow those people to think that we are inhospitable. Since this concerns the whole institution we hope to see all students, regardless of political feelings, unite in an effort to give our visitors a most hearty welcome. Let it be the aim of each student to do all in his power to make it pleasant for them. Let us give our friends such a hearty reception that they may long recall with pleasant thoughts the time when they attended the interstate contest at Lincoln.*

Hospitality and good conduct were established and carried over during the early years of football by educating the student fans through mass meetings on proper etiquette at games, then filtered through the stadium to all fans.

When football first appeared on campus, proper handling of the student body was crucial because very few fans had seen games and were unsure how to yell effectively, when to yell, and what to yell. A 1903 article stated, "A half dozen irresponsible persons shouting 'rotten' at decisions they did not understand could leave more impression than the great body of gentlemanly and intelligent, but organized students."

Early on, concerns about fan behavior prompted the University to take action, setting a precedence for today's standards and positive reputation of fan behavior at Cornhusker football games. Professor and Dean of the Law School Roscoe Pound (much more about him later) made this statement about fans: "They give an impetus to the team which no amount of coaching could supply. More than this, they unite the student body into an orderly and manageable band of 'rooters' making it easy to eliminate all rowdyism and promote good feelings at the game."

During the early years, students would yell the opposing school's yells. The University professors didn't feel this was appropriate and wanted to discourage this practice. It was considered good manners to only chant the yells that belonged to the University of Nebraska.

The University professors organized cheering sections in the stadium and cheerleading to assist in this endeavor. The cheerleaders had an important duty to help guide the student body and fans at the games, so they could be more effective in using appropriate cheers in different game situations, cheering in unison, and being loud to motivate the team on the field.

In fall 1901, University Chancellor E. Benjamin Andrews spoke at a mass meeting to discuss behavior of the student rooters. He was concerned about maintaining the good name and reputation of the University. Professor Wyer also spoke at the meeting and encouraged the students not to disturb the plays of the upcoming game with the Minnesota team by cheering while the play was in progress. Professor Wyer wanted to encourage fans to cheer between plays, since he felt that the action of cheering during a play was unbecoming of a gentleman.

At the meeting, the football team requested that all good plays by either side be applauded. This positive fan support is still on display today, as the University of Nebraska is known for their nice fans cheering for the opposing team. According to Michael Huckstep of the *Bleacher Report*, a letter was sent to the University of Nebraska from the former Florida State coach Bobby Bowden in 1980 after an 18–14 Seminoles victory in Lincoln, Nebraska:

> *I have been coaching college football the past 28 years and have played before some great crowds in this country. I have never seen people with more class than I saw at Nebraska last week. The Nebraska fans, players, cheerleaders, band, officials, coaches, etc., gave me a living testimony of what college football should be all about. I actually had the feeling that when we upset the Nebraska team that instead of hate and spite, the Nebraska fans thanked us for coming to Lincoln and putting on a good show. This is nearly unheard of in today's society. Nebraska, you are a great example for Americans to copy. I hope we show half the class your people do.*

Fan behavior was further shaped when action was taken in 1913 at an Innocents meeting. Professor George Condra was a huge sports fan and had helped establish the Innocents Society ten years earlier. According to author Robert Manley, "He

[Dr. Condra] did not care for the conduct of Nebraska students at football games, and he supported the Innocents Society as an agency which could educate the students in the proper ways of exhibiting school spirit."

Society members voted and approved to cheer for the opposing team when they came off the field, when a man was injured and came off the field, and at the end of the game. Today, these same behaviors from 1913 are witnessed in Memorial Stadium at any given home game. Another good gesture that became a tradition at Nebraska was for all students to remain standing while the players leave the field after the game. While standing, the students would join the band in singing "The Cornhusker."

An article in *The Daily Nebraskan* (the campus newspaper) from the 1920s mentioned that Nebraska fans were becoming known for their spirit. It stated, "Football experts are now taking the Nebraska morale and Nebraska spirit into consideration when they start to figure on the outcome of the Cornhusker games. Students, you are partly responsible for the state of affairs. Your unity, your pep, your sportsmanship, and your spirit have become part of every game." Also, "Nebraska declares that there are not any more loyal students in any university or college than students at the University of Nebraska."

On October 15, 1920, a fan behavior guideline was published in an editorial by *The Daily Nebraskan* editor, Orvin Gaston, which stated:

On The Gridiron

1. Rise and sing when the band plays "The Cornhusker."
2. Rise when the Cornhuskers or our opponents come on the field. Make a noise.
3. Applaud good plays whether made by Cornhuskers or opponents.
4. Always cheer the injured player.
5. Never criticize an official audibly.
6. Don't alibi. Congratulate the victory.
7. Watch the cheerleaders. Organized rooting is what puts spirit into the team.
8. Be loyal in defeat as well as in victory.
9. Remain standing until the team has left the field.

An editorial in *The Daily Nebraskan*, prior to the Kansas football game, was a reminder to the players and students concerning their behavior. The article stated, "Upon those who make the trip to the Jayhawker state will rest the responsibility of demonstrating the spirit and loyalty of the entire University. There is no necessity to define Nebraska spirit. It is based on the highest kind of good sportsmanship. Each individual who goes to Kansas, whether he be on the first team, the freshman squad, a member of the band, a 'Corncob' or an ordinary rooter, will help to contribute to that splendid spirit of which Nebraska is proud."

The article went on to state, "We must enact our parts as appreciative guests and show our southern friends that our student body is of a high caliber. Above all things show respect for their song or yell that is equivalent to our 'Cornhusker.' Nothing wins a warmer place in the heart of an opponent than a display of good sportsmanship."

Since the first football game in 1890, the students and fans would wait at the train station to celebrate the return of the football team from away games. When the Innocents took over the direction of cheerleading, they continued to encourage students and fans to be at the train station to greet the team when they returned. The society felt it was even more important to welcome the team back after a loss to show the players that the students were still backing them.

Also, during the 1920s, the University of Nebraska students would welcome opposing teams to Lincoln, holding a rally outside of their opponent's hotel the night before the game. This welcoming celebration started with a pep rally on campus at the Armory. The students would then march in a torchlight parade to the Lincoln Hotel where the opposing team was staying. The Corn Cobs, an all-male student pep organization, assisted the Iron Sphinx members, an all-male honors society, in forming the parade and leading the march. At the Lincoln Hotel, the president of the Innocents presided while the football captain and head coach gave speeches.

One such welcoming pregame pep rally on the eve of the football game happened on November 9, 1923. The opponents were the Fighting Irish of Notre Dame, and their head coach, the legendary Knute Rockne, was called upon to speak. In addition, the Irish football player and captain, Brown, introduced his team members. The Nebraska students led yells and songs for the Notre Dame players. The Corn Cobs bearing torches formed an "N" on the post office lawn and unfolded a large banner stating, "Welcome Notre Dame."

Despite the efforts made by the Nebraska students to welcome the Notre Dame team, an editor at the Irish paper, *The Notre Dame Daily*, wrote an article accusing Nebraska of being a poor host. This article made students at Nebraska determined to be even more welcoming to the next opponent, Syracuse.

The campus newspaper encouraged more students to participate and hoped that 5,000 students would come out and sing "Alma Mater," the Syracuse school song, and be a part of the welcoming program at Nebraska. In an article, Coach Fred Dawson (who was also dean of men) expressed, "A wish to have the 'orange' welcomed by every student, to have every student preserve the behavior of a gentleman—to the utmost."

Also, during this time at a pep rally, Head Coach Dawson and Line Coach Schulte gave speeches about the spirit that has made Nebraska "among the most courteous and sportsmanlike institutions in the country." In his speech, Coach Dawson declared, "We are going out to beat Syracuse. The team is representative of you and in order to win we must have your feeling behind us in heart and soul and boost, boost, boost."

Shortly after the Innocents Society was formed in 1903, mass meetings to teach game etiquette were no longer necessary. The Innocents created freshman convocations for incoming freshmen, both men and women, so they could learn proper fan behavior and school spirit. The freshmen would learn Nebraska school songs and yells, as well as the traditions of the University. The yell leaders were present to give the freshman their first knowledge of real Nebraska school spirit.

Once the school colors were officially changed to scarlet and cream in 1895, the colors would figure prominently on game day and be proudly displayed. At the games, the gentlemen would wear red neckties. Also, a fashionable accessory was a walking cane tied with ribbons of the school colors that fluttered in the breeze for added effect. Even unusual apparel was at times spotted at games, such as a half-red and half-white vest or red fez hats with white tassels, to support the colors of the school. Between 1945 and 1960, Golds Department Store in downtown Lincoln handed out, free to fans, a red feather with a white "N" to display on a hat.

THE SEA OF RED

The massive display of the color red worn into Memorial Stadium by the fans has long been referred to as the Sea of Red. This tradition of wearing school colors started quite early and solidified when an article in 1910 stated, "A special rooters' section will be reserved in the south bleachers at the Ames game tomorrow and only those will be admitted who wear colors and who are equipped with megaphones."

Again, in 1913 *The Daily Nebraskan* encouraged students and fans to wear the school color red into the stands for the game. In 1914, the male and female student rooting sections were required to wear scarlet caps. The caps were available for purchase at Magee's Clothing Store for twenty-five cents. The idea of wearing red caps was inspired by Stanford University where they had been worn since 1902. It was believed, "A scheme like this would work very well in Nebraska, every rooter to have a cap of the same design and used at all games. Having the caps made up in red, the rooting sections would present a blaze of color not obtainable in any other manner."

Starting in 1925, the Cornhusker team doctor, Dr. Dexter Dana King, of York, Nebraska, traveled with the football team on away games. Legend has it that Dr. King owned a red necktie; however, he refused to wear it until Nebraska beat Pittsburgh. Dr. King traveled with the team to Pittsburgh for twelve years from 1927 to 1939, each time packing his red necktie. He was unable to wear it until 1939 when the Cornhuskers beat Pittsburgh, at which time he immediately and proudly put on his red tie, a red felt hat, and red mittens. At Christmas that year, Dr. King gave every player and coach a red necktie in celebration of their victory.

Carrying on the school color tradition, the Cornhusker faithful continue to fill their home stadium with the color red and have made their presence known by wearing red in opposing stadiums.

SELLOUTS AT EVERY GAME

The passion of the Cornhusker fans continues to break NCAA records for consecutive sellout attendance (now with a stadium that holds approximately 90,000 game goers) that started on November 3, 1962, and was celebrated on September 26, 2009, when the 300th consecutive sellout was achieved. This sellout streak continues today with more than 361 games by November 24, 2017, and still counting.

"It's a great statement about the passion that their fan base has for their team and it's something that we're building here," Rutgers coach Kyle Flood said of Nebraska's sellout streak. "We're starting to see the beginning stages of it. They've been doing it for a long time out there. And it's a credit to the passion that their fans have and the loyalties that their fans have."

The loyal Nebraska fans are also known for following their team to away games. In 1901, at a cost of $3.00 per person, more than 3,000 fans accompanied the team to Minnesota. Current examples of this support were shown in 2000 when Cornhusker fans took over the majority of the Notre Dame stadium, and again on January 3, 2002, when 60,000 fans traveled to Pasadena for the 88th Rose Bowl game against the Miami Hurricanes. In 2001, President George W. Bush said, "I can't go without saying how impressed I am by the Nebraska fan base. Whether it be for women's volleyball or football, there's nothing like the Big Red."

Husker Nation Tailgate Party

In anticipation of Saturday football game days, fans stream into Lincoln early to mill around the campus or gather downtown, at the railyard, or in Lincoln's historic Haymarket district to talk football and in the distance hearing random shouts of "Go Big Red." The fans set up their tailgates surrounding the stadium and branching out in all directions. Tailgating brings Husker fans together before the game and is a place where family and friends can gather and share their Husker spirit.

On Saturday, August 30, 2003, prior to the home football game, former athletic director Steve Pederson debuted a new fan tradition called Husker Nation. The new tradition was designed by the University to honor the fans of the Cornhusker State who have made Husker athletics what it is today.

Three hours before kickoff on game days, the Husker Nation Pavilion is set up on the Ed Weir Track by Memorial Stadium to provide the largest tailgate party with food, live music, activities, and a jumbo television screen. As a thank you to the fans, the event offers free admission. In keeping with the gracious, best college football tradition, the opposing team's fans are welcomed as well. Also, at the debut of the tailgate, a bigger, buffer Herbie Husker mascot was unveiled, who it was felt was more representative of the Cornhusker fan.

The Cornhusker fan support goes beyond the home and away games. The fan attendance at the annual Red and White Spring Game is a national phenomenon. Nebraska broke a school record in 2008 with 80,149 fans in attendance of the spring game—one of the largest in college football history. With the hiring of a new head coach, Scott Frost, the spring game previous attendance record was shattered with 86,818 hopeful fans attending on April 21, 2018.

The outstanding reputation of the Cornhusker fan continues, when in November 2015, Brett McMurphy, an ESPN college football analyst, conducted a survey, polling college football coaches on the most knowledgeable fans. Not surprisingly, the Nebraska fans topped the chart at number one. McMurphy had this to say about the Cornhusker faithful: "Husker fans are also widely considered to be the 'nicest' in the sport as well, and perhaps the two categories go hand-in-hand."

In summary, the early University chancellor and professors were instrumental in setting and establishing decorum on proper behavior at games that was fit for a fine University. The University faculty knew from the beginning that tradition inspires performance, and that spark was ignited in the Nebraska student and fan. The tone set for Cornhusker fans in the early twentieth century is still felt today in Memorial Stadium on game day.

A 1920s article in *The Daily Nebraskan* noted, "The collegiate world asks, 'What sort of men and women are those at Nebraska?' Our spirit shall be the answer." And former Nebraska linebacker and sportscaster Trev Alberts once said, "Before you can move forward, you need to know where you've been." Thus, the legacy surrounding the spirit, loyalty, and traditions of the Cornhuskers, the Big Red, and the Husker Nation continues.

SIS-BOOM-AHH — YELL SQUAD SKYROCKETS TO POPULARITY

CHEERLEADING AT FOOTBALL GAMES HAD ITS "ROOTS" ON THE EAST COAST, AT Princeton University, the birthplace of American football. In the 1870s, it was only natural that cheering would originate there with student pep clubs and cheering sections in the stadium. The first Princeton cheer was borrowed from a military cheer called the "skyrocket" of the New York Seventh Regiment. The cheer could be heard as the soldiers sat in their railroad cars at the Princeton train station awaiting travel to Washington, on their way to the Civil War.

The Alumni Association of Princeton University reported, "In 1861, a regiment bound for battle in the Civil War passing through Princeton captivated the College's students with its 'skyrocket' cheer, which imitated the sound of fireworks—'sis' for the zooming rockets; 'boom' for the explosion; and 'ahhhh' as the crowd expressed its pleasure for the resulting light show."

In the 1880s, Princeton student and pep club member, Thomas Peebles, rounded up six men to lead a yell of "Sis Boom Rah!" in the student section for the first organized yell. The Princeton skyrocket cheer eventually evolved into their familiar locomotive cheer. Peebles graduated from Princeton in 1882 and moved to Minnesota in 1884 where he introduced the idea of chanting to spectators at the University of Minnesota.

The University of Minnesota Gophers were having a dismal football season in 1898. Through Peebles's influence, at a Minnesota game on November 2, 1898, a first-year medical student named Jack "Johnny" Campbell garnered attention by jumping out on the field in front of the football crowd to lead cheers and motivate the football team to victory.

"Someone needs to lead the yells with organized cheering," he shouted. The University of Minnesota won the game 11 to 6, and the value of cheerleading was recognized and validated when shortly after Campbell's initial cheer, the University of Minnesota appointed a squad of six male students to lead cheers at future games. Johnny Campbell led this cheer:

**RAH, RAH, RAH!
SKU - U - MAR, HOO - RAH! HOO - RAH!
VARSITY! VARSITY! VARSITY,
MINNESOTA!**

That moment in 1898 is considered the birth of cheerleading, by leading the fans in cheers from the field. In memory of Campbell's first cheer, a variation is still performed today at Minnesota games.

University of Minnesota's Johnny Campbell, their first cheerleader.

According to the University of Minnesota's *Daily Gopher*, "In 1904 cheerleading at the U of M was made official, and Campbell was crowned 'rooter king.' As for Johnny Campbell he attended every home game for 42 years, yelling the whole damn time."

As cheerleading was quickly spreading, cheering on the football team became as competitive as the athletes on the playing field. According to Pamela Bettis and Natalie Adams, authors of *Cheerleader! Cheerleader! An American Icon,* "As more and more colleges offered intercollegiate football, the need for institutional identity and proving one's loyalty to one's schools became intensified. Mascots, school colors, and local cheers helped to solidify this identity and loyalty to one's local schools." They went on, "Ultimately, the job of the cheerleader is to rally all of the school's citizens to support the team against the week's opponents. This is the heart of patriotism—to galvanize people to come together to support a common goal through the use of symbols, rituals, and traditions."

Professor Roscoe Pound was exposed to the excitement of football and cheerleading his one year at Harvard during the 1889–1890 football season. He returned to Lincoln in 1890 full of enthusiasm for the game of football and the support of cheerleading. Pound was considered the University of Nebraska's most enthusiastic fan and first unofficial cheerleader. He was professor of law in 1899 and became dean of the law school from 1903 to 1907, but he began writing and leading cheers and songs starting in 1890, in support of Nebraska's first football game and attended Nebraska's first away game on a field in Omaha, lending his cheerleading expertise.

During the first football game, the Nebraska fans gave their support to the team with continuous yelling and cheering, vibrating the grandstands. Every fan's hand waved pennant flags filling the air with the school colors. The noise and

Princeton graduate, Thomas Peebles, introduced organized cheering sections to the University of Minnesota in 1884.

the color the Nebraska fans brought to Omaha seemed to take over the town. *The Hesperian* (the school newspaper name until 1895 when it was changed to *The Nebraskan* until 1899, and then evolved to today's *The Daily Nebraskan*) reported after the game, "Pound, '88, was the most enthusiastic man of our party. He originated the flag scheme, and covered himself with glory, by composing the classical songs by which we entertained the common people on the way home from Omaha and persisted in singing them until we had a whole [train] coach to ourselves."

Pound had composed two songs in Latin and sang vigorously in celebration of Nebraska's first season game and first win. His enthusiasm spilled over to the crowd until all were loudly singing and celebrating the win. Organized cheering was considered as exciting as the football game, and the more noise, the better, to spur the team to victory. Wearing the colors of the school and noise produced by foghorns, bugles, megaphones, and cowbells were commonplace. At a game on November 5, 1897, the University had in place five squads of organized rooters.

It was reported, "Thanks to Roscoe Pound for his timely assistance. Mr. Pound was the prime mover of the organized rooting."

When football first began at the University of Nebraska, mass meetings were critical to involve the students. Mass meetings were held on campus to educate students on rules of the game, to organize yelling, to generate enthusiasm, to establish standards for behavior, to organize rallies, to generate ideas, and to pass a hat for fund-raising. From 1871 to 1903, the professors were the organizers and leaders on campus and would call the mass meetings to order. Pound's experience and enthusiasm quickly crowned him as the authority concerning rooting at the University. On December 1, 1903, Roscoe Pound wrote an article for *The Daily Nebraskan*:

> *Many of the new students had never heard of football, and few of the old students were not sure that they knew a punt from a place kick, or a touchback from a touchdown. Those who had athletics at heart preached, and exhorted, and told stories… the value of such outbursts as followed the Minnesota game last year and preceded and followed the Kansas game this year can hardly be overestimated. They give an impetus to the team which no amount of coaching could supply. More than this, they unite the student body into an orderly and manageable band of "rooters" making it easy to eliminate all rowdyism and promote good feeling at the games. In an ultra-democratic school, where everyone is potentially a leader, and congenital impatience of orders is tampered only by the military department, proper handling of the student body at the games has been a delicate undertaking. Very few have ever seen games at other institutions. Many have still to learn how to yell effectively, when to yell and at times, one is moved to think, what to yell. For want of proper handling, the mass of our students in years past have failed to make themselves felt. A half dozen irresponsible persons shouting "rotten" at decisions they did not understand, could leave more impression than the great body of gentlemanly and intelligent, but organized students. This year, there has been a great and wholesome change. The leadership has been good, and reasonably thorough. But much remains to be done, not merely to improve but to keep to the point that has been reached.*

In the spring of 1903, *The Daily Nebraskan* debated the issue of college spirit at football games. The faculty felt that there was not a lack of school spirit, but a lack of organized expression. Earlier attempts to cheer at games were, at times, successful, but there was a lack of consistency and stability. It seemed to the University professors that a more unified expression might be the key to enhancing school spirit at football games.

THE INNOCENTS SOCIETY FORMS

The solution was found in April 1903, when the Innocents Society was formed, and the students took over the role of organizing cheering. Professors Pound and George Condra had the idea to create the Innocents Society, a new senior honor society to take charge of leadership on campus. The society was created with the belief that a small group of intelligent men would be the leaders on campus, to organize enthusiasm and spirit.

Clark E. Bell, Innocents Society member and first head cheerleader, 1903.

Louis P. Hewitt, Innocents Society member and first of two cheerleaders on the all-male squad, 1903.

In September 1903, the Innocents Society officially organized the male cheerleaders on campus and took charge of the cheerleading going forward. During this September meeting, the Innocents appointed two of their own: Louis P. Hewitt as cheerleader and Clark E. Bell as head cheerleader. Since the Innocents were an all-male, senior honor society, this appointment resulted in the University of Nebraska having only males on their cheer squad, which mirrored all college cheerleading squads during this time. Establishing a leadership organization in charge of the cheerleaders was key to the successful organization of cheering at the University.

The new formation of a cheerleading squad was put into action and reported by *The Daily Nebraskan* on October 6, 1903. Captain Bell was in charge of leading the rooting and used a megaphone to inspire the Nebraska football team to victory. It was reported, "This was the first attempt at organized rooting for the year and was well conducted. What the men should learn, however, is to obey the leader implicitly. By this means the yells could begin in unison and everybody knows this is a better way than by scattered outbursts all along the line."

The cheerleading squad was transformed year after year to improve and evolve, to advance spirit and enthusiasm, and to be the best. Between the years of 1903 and 1911, the Innocents appointed two cheerleaders from within their own society. Efforts were made to improve the quality of cheerleading by opening the opportunity to a wider range of candidates, so in 1912, the cheerleaders were chosen from a system of tryouts.

On November 25, 1911, an article written by Robert D. Hawley, a cheerleader and Innocent, appeared in *The Daily Nebraskan*. Hawley put forth his opinion of the importance of rooting, of including co-eds, and of a tryout system to find the best talent.

> *Organized rooting is typical of the college world. It is the channel through which the exuberant spirits of collegians find overflow. It is a vivid example of their loyalty to their college and their fellows. By a popular growth, it has attained a position in the sphere of college activities from which it will probably never be dislodged.... What makes football the greatest of all college sports? Is it entirely due to love of the game itself, and to the fact that the pride of America's young manhood partakes in it? I think not. Let these same men complete their college course and then go out and play on some athletic club football team. Let two such teams compete in a game; would the number of spectators be large? No. The spirit and enthusiasm lent to it by the thousands of yelling students has disappeared and one of the greatest assets has been removed from the game. It is the general atmosphere of loyalty and good fellowship brought about by the organized rooting of student bodies that, to a great extent, has made football what it is....*
>
> *Rooting, to be most effective, must be well organized. Unless it is so it will be no more effective than the scattered cheering at some professional athletic contest. It must be really sincere*

to lead the proper ring and effect. I do not believe that rooting need be profane to be most effective. The purest and cleanest spirits is not voiced by means of profanity.

Here at Nebraska it is a harder task to organize the rooters than at many schools. The students are not housed together in dormitories, but are scattered all over the city of Lincoln. "Nebraska Spirit" must be kept at a high pitch to overcome this obstacle. We are ahead of the other schools in the Missouri Valley in many other things. Why should we not lead in school spirit and rooting?

We hear it said, here and there, that Nebraska has no yells. Do you suppose that a Nebraska grad, returning to his alma mater to witness a gridiron contest would believe that he was once more at Nebraska if he did not hear old No. 1 peal forth from the bleachers? That yell has become a part of the school itself. We do not want too many yells. It is hard to perfect a large number of yells and I believe that if we concentrate our efforts on the yells we now have that they will prove in the future, as they have in the past, very effective. Sometime in the future we may be given a better yell, but in the meantime we should do our best with that we have.

The argument is sometimes advanced that co-education kills college spirit. In my opinion, this has been successfully refuted at Nebraska. This has been accomplished by giving the co-eds a section of the grandstand to themselves, and thus urging them to attend athletic contests. The spirit among the co-eds here this year has been great. It has urged the men to make greater efforts and thus has strengthened the spirit of the whole school....

Cheerleading is an art that some men are especially adapted for while others are not. I do not believe that in the past, this year among the others, that the most capable men have always been chosen for this position.

For the 1912 football season, three cheerleaders were chosen from tryouts, and they all continued to be Innocents. During 1916, cheerleader selection was again opened to tryouts, as open tryouts continued to prove to be an effective way to select the best talent. The candidates would try out during the first game, and the Innocents selected the new cheerleaders.

The Daily Nebraskan announced the tryouts and reported, "The position is a difficult one, and yet one of the most important to the University, for the value of organized rooting as a factor in winning football games has been demonstrated time and time again." Scott Brown and Leo Adler were named the new cheerleaders for the football season of 1916–1917.

This season brought up a recommendation by the Innocents to the athletic board: if a cheerleader's efforts merited it, they should receive a sweater with an emblem, with an "N," at the end of the season. Awarding letter sweaters to cheerleaders was already practiced at eastern universities. The athletic board recognized the important role the cheerleader played in good rooting and winning football games, so they voted to adopt this ruling. This was the first time letter sweaters and letters were awarded to cheerleaders at Nebraska.

Cheerleaders Chal "Tiny" Gellantly and R. K. "Rocky" Amerman at a 1913 football game.

ONLY MEN COULD APPLY— BUT NOT FOR LONG

Females were always allowed academic entrance to the University of Nebraska, but only men played football and staffed the first cheerleading squads.

The Victorian era prevented women from attending football games unless accompanied by a male escort. In the 1900s, football had become a dangerous sport and considered a game full of brutality. In the 1905 season, eighteen deaths and 149 injuries were related to football. During the early years of football, society generally viewed women as delicate creatures; not surprisingly, these societal pressures required female students to have a male escort as a buffer from the sport's brutality. The prospect of women in attendance at games was viewed as questionable, so the idea of women cheering on the field would have been an unimaginable thought.

During the Victorian era several factors prohibited females from cheerleading activities: men outnumbered women on campus; the attitude of the times was to keep women feminine; and there was discussion of unknown health effects of strenuous physical activity on women. Due to these prevailing attitudes, females were not accepted as cheerleaders on college campuses in general, until the 1920s. But the University of Nebraska was progressive when it came to females involved in cheerleading. Nebraska broke barriers for allowing women to cheer on the field with men the fall football season of 1917.

Cheerleaders U. Severin Harkson and Burke W. Taylor, 1915–1916 season.

The female students had an interest in football and became actively involved in organizing their own stadium cheering sections starting in the 1904 season. In the beginning the females would lead cheers within their grandstand sections, but were not allowed on the field to lead cheers. One of the female students in the section leading cheers was Ruth Whitmore, who was an example for younger sister Frances Whitmore, who would later become one of the first female cheerleaders on the field in 1917.

A female cheering section was supported by the athletic department's Earl "Fido" Eager. An article by Wally Provost from the *Omaha World-Herald* in 1971 headlined, "Eager Opened Gate for Co-ed Rooters." This article was based on Eager, who was a football manager for the University of Nebraska football team. He was also in charge of ticket sales for the football games.

In 1911, he supported the idea to allow a co-ed rooting section to increase ticket sales and offered tickets at a reduced price to encourage participation. Provost wrote, "That historic season was 1911. Eager's brainstorm no doubt eased the way for an N.U. 'first' in 1917—cheerleaders in skirts. The names have been lost in time, but R. M. 'Dick' Lamb, unofficial historian of the

National Football Foundation and Hall of Fame, said he had 'quite authoritative information that Nebraska was the first school to employ girl cheerleaders.'"

As it turns out, the names were not lost in time at all. The first female cheerleaders at the University of Nebraska (and the earliest female cheerleaders in college football history) were Frances Willard Whitmore, Mildred Gillilan, and Helen Miller Howe. And the story of how women took the field as cheerleaders is quite revealing about women's issues at the time.

Particularly, it was Louise Pound's effort to provide equal opportunity that brought about the first female cheerleaders to cheer on the field with the males at the University of Nebraska. With tryouts being opened to the student body, cheerleading soon became an opportunity for females and created another first for the University of Nebraska. (More about the profound influence Louise Pound has had on the University coming up. Yes, she is Roscoe Pound's sister, and those of you who attended the University will recall Pound Hall, a dorm named after Louise.)

As time went on, the athletic department and the Innocents began to question the appropriateness of women cheerleading on the field alongside men. In addition to cheerleading, the topic of women in athletics was raising several questions concerning the effects on the health of women, and if these activities were appropriate. The attitudes of Victorian era were making a comeback, and societal changes were coming to the forefront.

The athletic department, in conjunction with the Innocents, sent letters to other universities in the fall of 1921, asking if they had women cheerleaders. At an Innocents meeting on October 11, 1921, Dr. Wythers read telegrams from five other universities in regard to women cheerleaders. According to the meeting minutes, "All said that they do not have women cheerleaders at the football games."

It is not known which colleges the Innocents wrote their letters to, but what is known is that the Innocents would have been familiar with the teams they played in the Missouri Valley Conference and knew females did not cheer on the sidelines for these schools. Also, the athletic department and the administration at the University of Nebraska valued eastern college programs. Both all-male Princeton and Yale did not allow female students to even enroll until 1969, and it was this year that Yale allowed women to cheer. Also, Harvard did not allow admittance of women until 1977, however, their sister college, Radcliffe, provided female cheerleaders for the first time for a Harvard basketball game in 1970.

To this day, Texas A&M University has only an all-male cheer squad, which is now considered unique. The Innocents made the decision not to have women

Frances Willard Whitmore   *Mildred Gillilan*   *Helen Miller Howe*

The first three female college cheerleaders, not only at the University of Nebraska but in the nation, cheered on the field with male cheerleaders during the 1917-1918 season.

On the field, for the first time with female cheerleaders along with the males at this 1917 football game.

Cheering together at a 1918-1919 football game. (From left) Frances Willard Whitmore, Glen Wm. Hopkins, Helen Miller Howe, and Harry P. Troendly.

DEBRA KLEVE WHITE

Game day 1917, the first three female cheerleaders. (From left) Mildred Gillilan, Francis Willard Whitmore, and Helen Miller Howe.

First Nebraska female cheerleaders hold championship sign during game day, 1917.

In front of the sizable number of fans in the grandstand for a 1917 football game, cheerleaders. (From left) Francis Willard Whitmore, Helen Miller Howe, and Mildred Gillilan.

cheerleaders at the games starting the fall of 1921. A small article made the front page of *The Daily Nebraskan* in announcing female cheerleaders would no longer be allowed to cheer on the field. There is no record of a student response or if there was backlash from the decision to no longer allow female cheerleaders on the squad with the male cheerleaders. Despite this decision, the female students continued to support school spirit and the football team from their cheering section in the stadium.

Open tryouts continued as the method for selecting the new members of the cheerleading squad, and this selection process continues today. The faculty trained the cheerleader candidates on the principles of leading yells, and once the new cheerleaders were selected, the training classes taught proper skills to the new members of the squad. The cheerleaders were assigned to special sections of the stadium, and the assignments were changed from game to game. The tradition of rotating positions around the stadium is still carried on today to include participation of fans in all sections of the stadium.

1938 cheerleader Harry Kammerlohr.

Women Make a Comeback

From 1921 to 1943, the University of Nebraska cheerleading squad had remained all male. However, once again, the timing was right for female students to cheerlead at Nebraska. In the fall of 1942, after a twenty-three-year absence, the fans were pleased to see a Nebraska female cheerleader on the field at an away game. Her name was Janet "Jidge" Mason. According to conversations with John "Jack" Hogan, the Yell King at the time, and Jidge Mason, they recounted the event and how it unfolded. It was the 1942–1943 football season, and male students were being sent off to World War II. There were concerns of not having enough male students showing up for cheerleading tryouts.

All-male cheerleading squad, 1934: (Back row, from left) Whitey Reed, Dave Powell; (Front row, from left) Bob Pierce, Beverly Finkle (Yell King), and Bill Garlow.

Cheerleader with megaphone during 1925–1926 season, Phil Sidles.

(From left) Cheerleaders Hank Damkroger, Bernie Urich, Ike Walter, and Rollie Mangold, 1943.

A freshman reporter for *The Daily Nebraskan*, Janet "Jidge" Mason, decided to do a story on cheerleading tryouts. She was familiar with cheerleading at Nebraska because her brother John Mason had been a cheerleader during his 1939–1941 school years. In preparation for her story, Jidge Mason drove with the male cheerleaders to a football game on October 30, 1942, as Nebraska played the Jayhawks in Lawrence, Kansas. On the road, the cheerleaders were practicing their cheers and teaching the cheers to her. At the game, she borrowed a cheerleader jacket and cheered with the men on the field. According to Jidge Mason, "At the football field, the Nebraska fans went wild with cheers, seeing their first female cheerleader in action."

The next day after the game, the cheerleaders had arrived back on campus, and Yell King Jack Hogan and Jidge were called into the dean of women's office. They were promptly informed that the University did not allow female cheerleaders. This was a serious matter to be called into the dean's office. The students risked being expelled from school. The implication of being expelled would have been extremely detrimental for Hogan; however, he was a kind and caring person and was raised with the belief of equal rights for women. He did not let the risk outweigh what was right, and he stood up in support of women in cheerleading.

Considering the positive reaction from the crowd and standing up for what was right, Hogan made a proposal to the dean, and they struck a compromise. It was decided to let students vote and make the final decision on the fate of female cheerleaders. The outcome was positive, and the student body voted to allow women to cheer for the University of Nebraska.

According to Jidge Mason, recounting her brief moment cheering for the Cornhuskers, she decided not to try out in 1944 when tryouts were opened to women. She did not consider herself a real cheerleader. She was a student majoring in journalism and considered herself a newspaper woman. Yell King Jack Hogan bravely supported women in cheer and, with his belief in equal rights, helped pave the way to bring females back to the cheer squad at the University of Nebraska.

Cheering for Equal Rights

It was perfect timing for women to be included with the 1944 cheer squad. The female students could now fill the gaps as the male students were going off to war. Also, women in cheer during the 1940s were part of a national cultural shift in allowing women to be accepted in leadership roles in cheerleading and the following trends.

- Increasing numbers of female undergraduates on campus (making up 47% of the student body)

- Expansion of the Greek system and taking on leadership roles

- The role of the Miss America pageant in making beauty pageants popular

- The glamour of women in Hollywood and on the movie screen

Adding female cheerleaders back on the cheer squad was supported by the Nebraska students and the fans, after the positive reaction to Jidge Mason's cheering debut, and was now supported by the University administration. The

With females back on the squad in 1944 (the first since 1921): (bottom row, from left) Jackie Scott, Janet Krause, Doris Easterbrook, Anna "Hink" Aasen, (top row, from left) Ray Biemond, Bill Thompson, and Oscar Wisby being led by Yell King Bernie Urich.

Cheerleaders Cherie Viele and Betty Aasen pose in front of the Field House, 1948.

Female cheerleaders were reinstated on the squad for the 1944–1945 football season after an outcry from the students for equal representation. (From left) Jackie Scott and Anna "Hink" Aasen.

first females on the squad in 1944 were Anna "Hink" Aasen, Doris Easterbrook, Janet Krause, and Jackie Scott. The female addition brought about positive change and a renewed enthusiasm.

Oh, but what about those earlier concerns whether cheerleading was ladylike? This was demonstrated in 1944 during a pep rally parade when the cheerleaders were marching with the band. Cheerleader Anna "Hink" Aasen, in the excitement of the moment, performed a cartwheel, showing a glimpse of her cheer underpants. The next day Aasen was called before the dean of women to discuss her unladylike conduct. No action was taken, and Aasen continued to cheer, but no more cartwheels were allowed. The 1944 female cheerleaders cartwheeled into history and tested the rules as they forged new ground.

In fall 1949, Yell King and Innocents member Frank Piccolo recommended to the Innocents that the cheer squad should be composed of six men and six women, plus the Yell King. The Innocents approved the plan proposed by Piccolo. By the spring of 1950, discussions between the Innocents and Potsy Clark, athletic director, took place on how to improve the cheer squad. Also, by 1950, men were returning from war and sought to reclaim their positions on the cheer squad.

A cheerleader committee appointed by the Innocents was formed to analyze and review this matter, and the committee included Catherine Rapp, representative of the Tassels (a female pep organization); John Connelly, Innocent; Frank Piccolo, Yell King and Innocent; Col. Frankfurter, associate professor of chemistry and advisor to the Corn Cobs, Tassels and Band; Merle Stalder, president of Innocents; and Don Lentz, University ROTC band director. (More about the Corn Cobs and Tassels as part of the spirit of Nebraska coming up.)

The committee sent a questionnaire to fifteen other colleges throughout the country who were well known for cheering and school spirit to learn their method of governing the cheerleaders. Six of the schools had squads that consisted only of men. The cheerleading committee reviewed all responses from other colleges and after long discussions formulated a reorganized plan for the Yell Squad. The new plan included the formation of a Yell Squad advisory board that included the presidents of the Innocents, Corn Cobs, and Tassels, the director of athletics, Yell King, the gymnastic coach, speech instructor, and the band director.

And Then Back to an All-Male Squad

A unique feature of the new plan was the training program for the cheerleaders. It was the opinion of the Innocents that training would make Nebraska's squad one of the finest in the Midwest, which was their goal. During an Innocents meeting on November 13, 1950, the minutes showed, "The athletic board will take over the Yell Squad only if women are left out of the group—according to Potsy Clark. He says it would be impossible to handle women under the athletic setup that now exists in the Coliseum. We agreed." The committee decided to return to an all-male squad for the following reasons: easier to train in gymnastics and tumbling, the squad to become better acquainted with the team by visiting the locker room, less trouble traveling on out-of-state trips, and all men would make a more flexible squad.

A rally committee was formed to be in charge of all student pep rallies. The committee members consisted of two Corn Cobs, two Tassels, the Yell King, and a band member. This major cheerleading reorganization plan was adopted by the Innocents and approved by Potsy Clark. After the announcement of the new reorganization plan, Clark said it was the best move toward promoting a unified squad and successful cheering section since he had been at the University.

A decision was made to go back to an all-male squad of eight members who would be selected by a new Yell Squad advisory board. As part of the reorganization in 1950, this was the first year the cheerleaders were called the Yell Squad, which is how they are still known today, within the Spirit Squad organization. Throughout history the University of Nebraska, cheerleaders have been known as head rooters, cheerleaders, and Yell Squad.

The new, improved reorganization and training plan also included the first year a coach was assigned to the cheerleaders. Starting with the 1950 season, Jake Geier was named head coach of the Yell Squad, and Don Kline was named speech coach. Coach Geier was the new gymnastic head coach at the University and was the perfect person to lead the Yell Squad. Geier began coaching at the University of Nebraska in 1950 and had a long, successful career in gymnastics until he retired in 1969, and through the years compiled a record of 127–55 that included twenty gymnastics championships.

According to Geier, the athletic director asked him to step in and help out with coaching the Yell Squad. During his time as Yell Squad coach, he brought gymnasts to the football games to provide tumbling and entertainment for the fans. Coach Geier would recruit male gymnasts to see if they had an interest in performing at the football games. The gymnasts continued to be a part of the game through the 1960s performing tumbling, handstands on the goal posts, and using the springboard.

Cheerleaders used a springboard to count touchdowns. This is from a 1963 game.

In the 1950–1951 season, the cheerleaders introduced the springboard. The males would perform flips and jumps off it. When the females were added back to the squad in 1951, they jumped off the board with their arms stretched out in a "V" formation for victory. Also, the springboard was used to count the score after touchdowns.

The 1954 *Cornhusker* yearbook commented about the springboard count. "During the game, the 'automatic count' given by the Husker cheerleaders after every Nebraska touchdown is a happy moment for Nebraska fans." The springboard counting was used until the 1966–1967 season when it was replaced by the Yell Squad females performing a routine with pompons after a touchdown. At that time, the Yell Squad first started to coordinate school song routines and yells with the band.

Once Jake Geier was appointed as the Yell Squad coach, the Innocents Society was no longer involved with the squad, except to help select the Yell King. Coach Geier remained in this position as cheer coach until 1966. To this day, he held this position longer than any other coach in Yell Squad history.

The reorganization plan was created with good intentions to form the best Yell Squad to increase spirit. What the athletic department and the cheerleading committee didn't account for was the reaction of the students, especially the female students, vocalizing equal representation on the squad. This sentiment was demonstrated in a letter submitted to "Letterip" in *The Daily Nebraskan*, by seven sororities on campus (Delta Gamma, Pi Beta Phi, Chi Omega, Kappa Kappa Gamma, Gamma Phi Beta, Kappa Alpha Theta, and Alpha Phi):

> *This letter concerns a recent proclamation made by the Innocents Society. It concerns the recent change over to an all-male Yell Squad. This decision for an all-male Yell Squad was first made by a committee of students and administrators directly concerned with Nebraska pep and spirit. It was then voted on and carried by the Innocents Society, which is the sponsor of the Yell Squad.*
>
> *But, the main voice of the university, the student body, was not advised on the subject. We feel that such a decision should at least have been brought up before the students. We also feel that the decision was wrong because in a co-educational school, the co-eds should be represented in the Yell Squad as well as in every other campus function.*
>
> *The reasons given for the revision may be well founded, but a Yell Squad of three or four girls and four boys could also work well under correct organization. By correct organization we mean a sponsor, training, and cooperation from the whole student body.*

The main advice received from other state universities in a survey taken by the committee was speech training for the Yell Squad members. Gymnastics, the most outstanding feature of the new setup was in second place. If the Yell Squad needs gymnasts and gymnasts do add to a Yell Squad the boys could do that work, while speech training could be given to the whole squad—boys and girls.

Looking back on the history of Nebraska yell squads, we see that in 1940, an all-male squad was taken to the Rose Bowl game, and returned home with some high recommendations. But, had girls been along, it is sure bet that they would have returned home with the same recommendations. It takes a top team to make a top Yell Squad and it takes a top Yell Squad to make a top team.

First rally of the 1951–1952 season on the steps of the Coliseum.

This protest isn't lightly founded. For example, the N-club at a recent meeting found that "a majority of the members favored having at least three women on the squad."

The resurrection of the all-male squad only lasted one year. The 1951–1952 season brought back the females onto the cheerleading squad, and since this time females have remained continuously on the squad. Jack Geier recalled that the Yell Squad had been lacking without the females on the squad. The 1952 *Cornhusker* yearbook stated, "University students were happy again this year as the co-ed returned among the ranks of the cheerleader." The 1951–1952 Yell Squad consisted of three females and eight males. As the years progressed, the number of females grew to exceed the number of males on the squad.

Note the large pompons used by the cheerleaders in 1954. (Back row, from left) Don Orr, Charles Trumble, Don Beck; (Second row, from left) Don Fogel, Robert Green, Joan Pollard, Gene Christensen, Doris Jean Anderson; (Front row, from left) Carolyn Elliot and Marilyn Eaton.

BRING ON THE POMPONS AND THE PEP

The football season of 1954–1955 was the first time pompons were used in a game. The pompons were homemade by the members themselves, using crepe paper, and only used on a very limited basis, because the red color of the crinkly paper bled onto the cheerleaders.

The Carillon Tower was dedicated in 1949 and caused so much excitement and spirit on campus that two pep rallies were held. Also in 1954, a tradition showing spirit was reflected in the Carillon Tower, which would ring out loyalty songs over the campus at the end of every home game.

In the mid-1960s through the 1970s, the Yell Squad would line up at the opening of the stadium where the team would emerge for the game, firing up the fans and generating fan enthusiasm. When the team was ready to enter the field, the Yell Squad would run the football team onto the field with their pompons raised in the air, running the 100-yard distance and ending at the goal line with a school fight song routine. A version of the spirit lineup is used today during the pregame ceremonies, as the Spirit Squad lines up to welcome the team to the field, and some of the Yell Squad members carry large red flags spelling out "N-E-B-R-A-S-K-A", running the team onto the field.

In 1960, a Howitzer cannon was fired at football games after a touchdown.

In 1960, the University added a spirit cannon to the games to announce scoring by the Husker team. The cannon, a 75-millimeter Howitzer, was requisitioned from the Army for the University. The Innocents were in charge of the safety and the firing of the cannon. Feedback was received that the noise of the cannon was annoying, and there were reports the press box would shake when the cannon was fired. The cannon's position was moved from time to time to find the optimal location, but the cannon did not remain a tradition.

Coach Geier was instrumental in transforming the Yell Squad heading into the 1963 season for the most dramatic change in sixty years. Geier wanted to get more crowd participation at games so he decided to change his philosophy by adding more entertainment. He initially approached the Tassels to form a dance group, but it did not materialize. Coach Geier took matters into his own hands and envisioned and created a pompon squad at the University of Nebraska. The group did not have a name; they were simply known as pompon girls or pompon squad.

During the spring of 1963 at the Yell Squad tryouts, it was not mentioned that a separate pompon squad was going to be formed. Tryouts were very simple. Students had to perform a couple basic cheers—"Go Big Red" was one of them. According to Coach Geier, the girls were called up to the judge's table and they had to run up and say their name. Their ability to run up to the table was 50 percent of the qualifications on how they were chosen. There were thirteen openings, plus an alternate, chosen for the cheerleader squad. The groups were then split into Yell Squad and pompon squad. Originally six women were assigned to the pompon squad from tryouts. The women assigned to the pompon squad were Sandra Stepfanism, Georgia Merriam, Becky Haas, Linda Keating, Jean Barber, and Sandra Lane.

A Nebraskan, Carolyn Daubert had transferred to the University of Nebraska after spending her first three semesters at Colorado State University (CSU). While at CSU, Daubert was a member of the Pepperettes, a pompon squad, which today is known as the Golden Poms. One of the members of the new University of Nebraska pompon squad was a sorority sister with Daubert. She knew Daubert had been a pompon girl at CSU and invited her to the new pompon squad's practice.

Until Daubert arrived at practice, the pompon squad had a difficult time coming up with a basic dance step. Originally it was called a skip, done to a one-two count, and since has been referred to as "the step." Carolyn Daubert showed the new pompon squad the step footwork and some of the routines that the Pepperettes had performed at CSU. The step was brought to the University in 1963 and perfected into the 1970s as a unique style as the official footwork of the Yell Squad.

The 1966 Oklahoma State football game featured the Yell Squad showing the Nebraska image in a nationwide televised broadcast. The female squad members included Sally Cockle, Barb Doan, Maggie Evenson, Kathy Henderson, Meredith Hester, Jeanine Howard, Kitty McManus, and Judy Switzer.

The step did not last at CSU. Yet the step has become a treasured tradition with the Nebraska Yell Squad and is still performed today. The step evolved to a simpler version in the 1990s as more focus was placed on partner stunting.

After working with the squad for a couple of practices, Daubert was asked to join the group. Therefore, the football season of 1963–1964 consisted of a male and female Yell Squad and a separate seven-member female pompon squad.

The Yell Squad has always had a Yell King leader, so Geier decided to have a spokeswoman or captain of the pompon squad. Geier determined it was easier to hear suggestions or complaints from one voice instead of eight. Later when the two squads were combined, Yell Squad continued the tradition of a male Yell King and a female captain.

The new pompon squad did not select their uniforms, but had some input. More than likely it was Jake Geier who was in charge of the uniform selection.

The uniform of the pompon squad included a V-neck sweater made of wool, with bold, vertical strips of scarlet and cream worn over a button-down collared, white oxford shirt, and a cream-colored wool, pleated skirt landing above the knee, white bobby socks, and white tennis shoes. An emblem was not necessary because the uniform had a distinct look and was recognizable as representing the University of Nebraska.

The next year black-and-white saddle shoes were incorporated as standard footwear with the uniform. When saddle shoes were added to the uniform, they made a fashion statement to little girls who wanted to be like the pompon squad, and there was a run on department stores for the purchase of saddle shoes. The pompon squad utilized large mixed red-and-white paper pompons to move through their new and unique routines and dances. The 1963 pompon squad was new, fresh, and stylish, and their uniform and style provided a unique look from other college squads. Upon their debut, they became an instant hit with the Nebraska fans for their classy new style.

The pompon squad performed routines to "No Place," "Hail Varsity," and several dance routines to band music. The squad developed their own choreography to the school songs and dances. They helped form the spirit lineup when the team ran onto the field. Also, they performed dances at a few half-time shows with the band. During the game the pompon squad always performed when the band played; however, they did not lead the crowd in cheers. Leading the cheers was the responsibility of the Yell Squad.

Due to the pompon squad's popularity, it was determined by the next school year to combine the cheerleaders and pompon females into one squad as the Yell Squad and adopt the pompon squad's uniform and routines. The 1964 squad was the first year the squad was a combination of a cheer and pompon/dance squad and continued with dual duties until 1992.

Tryouts and practices took place on the University's Coliseum stage and in 1979 moved to Mabel Lee Hall. As a warm-up regimen, a recording of the song "Chicken Fat" by Robert Preston, a youth fitness song, would play at the beginning of each practice session to walk the squad through warm-up exercises. The recorded song became outdated and no longer used by the start of the 1980 season.

The new squad was so popular with the Cornhusker fans, a commemorative drinking glass was created with an image of a squad member to celebrate the 1971–1972 football championship seasons. The image on the glass bears the likeness of Carolyn Daubert, from the original 1963 pompon squad. Also, to commemorate the 1971–1972 seasons, a pull-string talking cheerleader doll was created by Mattel as a promotional item.

During the 1979–1980 season, the Yell Squad performs a pyramid at a basketball game. Yell Squad members: (Front row kneeling) Sally Pearson (Captain); (Middle row, from left), Debra Kleve, Scot Cockson, Griff Davenport (Yell King), Russ Hoffbauer, Lee Chapin, Liz Held; (Back row on shoulders, from left) Patti Charvat, Karen Kirwan, Deneé Nelson, Sandy Perkins, Kim Welsh.

Yell Squad members Geri Finney and Todd Wheeler perform a lift at the Kansas game on November 16, 1985.

The Yell Squad practices spelling "N-E-B-R-A-S-K-A" with their poms, getting ready for game time, 1979–1980 season.

In 1972, the females changed their skirt from cream to a red pleated wool. They also changed their pompons to one all red and one all white paper pompons.

Large plastic pompons were incorporated for basketball after 1974 in order to prevent the shedding of paper on the court. The larger plastic pompons were too heavy for use in the routines, so gloves were used, originally all white and changed to one side red and one side white to make hand movements stand out. The pompons used for football became smaller in size in 1992, and changed from paper to plastic.

Sky-high Stunts and Signs

1996 Yell Squad stunting on the field at Memorial Stadium.

A mini trampoline was incorporated in early 1971, but was no longer being used by the mid-1970s. The squad started performing a few cheerleading lifts in the early part of the 1970 season, and through the 1970s, several lifts and pyramids were incorporated with the performances.

Also, mid-1970s brought about the first use of large signs to engage the fans in cheering. The signs were first used at basketball games displaying "Go Big Red" and letters spelling out "Huskers," and later used at football games for a competitive battle among the fans of "Husker" and "Power."

Already in place in the 1970s, the Yell Squad had a candy box tradition. The Yell Squad would greet and welcome the opposing cheerleaders at each home football game. The University of Nebraska Yell Squad would decorate the outside of a box with the opposing team's colors and fill it with red candy. There was always a positive reaction to the red candy by the opposing cheerleaders. The tradition was a gesture to help make the opposing cheerleaders feel welcome. The candy box tradition ended the fall season of 1980.

The style of the Yell Squad's uniforms became a tradition and continued for fifteen years until the uniform was changed for the 1978–1979 season. Leading up to this season, the squad's uniform became a topic of conversation. Some of the fans were vocal in wanting a new uniform for the Yell Squad for an updated look, while other fans liked the traditional style. The end of an era came in the fall of 1978, when the striped uniforms were no longer worn.

The consensus of the squad was to sport a unique look to distinguish the Nebraska Yell Squad from other cheer squads. The new uniforms appeared at the first football game of 1978 to mixed reactions from the students and fans. Some fans still liked

1996 Yell Squad on the field.

the traditional style and thought the new uniforms were too white. Others thought it was refreshing, updated, and liked the new look. The uniform lasted one season and since then the uniforms have frequently changed during subsequent seasons.

During 1977–1980, the female Yell Squad used their pompons to create letters to spell out words, using signs to spell out words, and the Yell Squad males spelled out letters with their bodies on the football field.

By the late 1970s, national cheerleading, dance camps, and competitions were becoming popular. In the summer of 1978, the Yell Squad attended the National Cheerleaders Association (NCA) camp in Dallas and returned home an award-winning squad having received a superior rating (the highest award)

1997 Yell Squad performing a sky-high basket toss.

Yell Squad Captain Sally Pearson cheered with one pompon during the fall football season after breaking her elbow (pictured here at the 1979 Utah State game).

Spirit Squad giving back to the community, October 21, 2012.

for their routines. The squad also brought home two trophies—one for overall performance and another for the best home routine.

National cheerleading competitions gained in popularity, and partner stunting became a necessity, so stunting began to evolve at Nebraska. During the season of 1980–1981, the number of females and males was equal at the University, which aided in performing partner stunts. By 1982, students with gymnastic ability were encouraged to try out. The Yell Squad was emerging into the sport of cheerleading, which was becoming the latest trend of cheering.

The Nebraska Yell Squad was developing into a competitive and award-winning squad. Between 1984 and 1998, the squads were finalists as one of the top twenty cheerleading squads in the National Cheerleaders Association College Cheerleading Championships. The season of 1988-1989 they placed seventh. The 1989-1990 year they placed fourth. The season of 1990-1991 the Yell Squad was one of four squads selected to cheer at the 1991 Japan Bowl in Tokyo. In 1996, the Yell Squad performed during the summer Olympics opening ceremonies. In the 1995–1996 season the Spirit Squad went to nationals, and the Yell Squad placed fifth. The 1996–1997 Spirit Squad again placed at nationals in 1997 at NCA in Daytona Beach, Florida, with Yell Squad placing second.

It was clear by the 1990s that the Yell Squad was performing at some of their highest levels in competition and was considered one of the finest squads in the country.

The Yell Squad's purpose was to represent the University as public relations personnel, along with generating spirit and support for athletic

1978-1979 Award-Winning Yell Squad at NCA camp in Dallas, Texas. (Front row, from left) Karen Kirwan, and Sally Pearson; (Second row, from left) Julie O'Meara, Patti Charvat, Sandy Perkins, and Griff Davenport; (Third row, from left) Deb Kleve, Susan White, John Slavens, and Liz Held; (Back Row, from left) Chris Lofgreen, and Tim Holscher.

events. The Yell Squad members make approximately 200 appearances at athletic, community, and statewide events. This is accomplished as full-time students, along with squad conditioning and practice several hours a week, all the while maintaining high scholastic standards. Today the Spirit Squad has many responsibilities on game day, but overall they consider themselves ambassadors for the University.

As cheerleading was moving toward being classified as a sport, it incorporated gymnastics, stunts, and tosses. The stunts continued to increase in difficulty for fan entertainment and for national competitions, which has elevated the level of risk. Injury has always been a part of cheerleading, as with any sport. The increased stunting level brings with it increased risk and potential for injury.

Injury Grounds the Yell Squad

The injury risk hit home at the University of Nebraska in 1996 when a female cheerleader was seriously injured outside of cheerleading practice, but on University property. A resulting lawsuit was settled in 2001, when the University agreed to a $2.1 million settlement. Athletic Director Bill Byrne announced the Yell Squad would be "grounded" starting with the 2002 season due to the risk to the student members and liability to the University.

Bill Byrne announced in March 2002 that he was ground bounding the cheerleading squad beginning in the fall 2002, meaning they "could not perform pyramids or stunts. The policy prohibits cheerleaders from performing any exercises in which both feet and both hands leave the floor. Not only does such a policy prohibit the squad from building pyramids, performing partner stunts, and doing advanced tumbling; if taken literally, it also prohibits them from even jumping." Unfortunately, injuries are a part of the sport of cheerleading, and with the increase of stunts and tosses, so has the risk and danger increased.

On January 1, 2003, a new athletic director, Steve Pederson, was hired by the University. As it was announced on February 11, 2003, Pederson would be relaxing the ban on the grounding of the Yell Squad, due to fan feedback. "Pederson said a visible active cheer squad traditionally had been an integral part of Nebraska athletic events. Thus, Pederson is allowing low-risk routines—ones where cheerleaders maintain contact or are stacked one-high. Tumbling, pyramids and basket tosses are still not allowed."

Stunting involves the men lifting the women above their heads with their hands and this was allowed. The announcement came as good news to the Yell Squad members and the fans. However, it was short-lived, as once again starting the season of 2007, Pederson made a decision to ground the Yell Squad. The decision was made based on growing, overall safety concerns.

In 2007, the cheer coach, Carrie Krenk Jansen, had the idea to re-create the traditional bold-striped uniforms, which had been worn in the 1960s and 1970s. The retro uniforms were worn at a couple of football games and during some of the basketball games the first year they were reintroduced. The crowd reaction was very favorable and brought about the memories of a beloved Yell Squad style. The vintage-style sweater of the past was worn for special occasions to generate enthusiasm with the fans and honor the past Yell Squad tradition.

What drew the male student to the sport of cheerleading has always been the stunting. The grounding of the Nebraska cheerleaders diminished the interest of males in the activity of cheerleading. During the football season of 2007–2008, two male Yell Squad members, Zach Hergert and John Clabaugh, were part of the squad. With the start of the 2008–2009 season, John Clabaugh came back in a volunteer position to run the Nebraska flag at the football games, as the final male Yell Squad member of a long, proud legacy of male cheerleaders. The following season during spring tryouts, no men were awarded a position on the squad; therefore, the fall of 2009 was the first time in the 106-year history that men were not a part of the Yell Squad.

Cheerleading has experienced a role reversal over the last 125 years, starting with all-male squads while today the majority of squads are female, and the University of Nebraska squad is currently all female. When cheerleading originated as a male-only activity, it was considered masculine and attracted the leaders on campus. As cheer evolved and females took over the role, the feminization of cheerleading increased. Males in the activity found it necessary to defend their participation. The males were subjected to questions about their masculinity. The males responded to these questions with remarks of having the best job on campus because they work with and lift the female cheerleaders or they would carry a football and throw it around at practice and on the sidelines at games.

In the 1990s, as cheer evolved into a sport requiring strength and masculinity, questions and tension eased for the male cheerleaders, and, as a result, cheerleading moved into being considered a sport involving athleticism, strength, and power. Cheerleaders have been considered American cultural icons, and over the years cheerleading has evolved to accommodate changing cultural norms, beliefs, and to continue to promote spirit, fan entertainment, and enhance the game day experience.

A Tradition of Enthusiasm

Since 1890, the football field has created unity for the University, the Spirit Squad, the students, fans, and the whole state of Nebraska, where traditions have been born and bred. Many of the sacred traditions have lived on: the Tunnel Walk, balloon release, sellout streak, touching the horseshoe, Blackshirts, and the school songs. However, many traditions have been lost to the dust of time. As time marches on, new traditions are created to boost game day excitement and enthusiasm.

With cheerleading, the only certainty is change. Through innovation, creativity, and style, the University of Nebraska's Yell Squad and Spirit Squad have provided entertainment, tradition, and enthusiasm, and have successfully brought together and led the student body and Cornhusker fans. The goals set by the first squad in 1903, and all Yell Squad members past and present, have established and continue to carry on a true Spirit of Nebraska.

Of course, cheerleaders would have nothing to cheer about or tradition to build on if it weren't for the popularity of the East Coast game of football. The University of Nebraska struggled to plant itself in the capital city of Lincoln, Nebraska, in the late 1800s, and campus athletic events burgeoned, as the first football game was played. As students began to understand the odd game, they started cheering for their home team. Many of today's football traditions surrounding cheerleading and the spirit of Nebraska began over a century ago on a muddy field with one odd-shaped ball and a growing interest in a ragtag team without a name or a loyal following.

3

The Beginning of Nebraska Football, School Spirit, and the Ushering in of Cheerleading

The year was 1869. The University of Nebraska was founded in the state capital city of Lincoln, and concurrently the first intercollegiate football game was played between Rutgers and Princeton. But it wasn't until November 27, 1890, that the first football game kicked off at Nebraska.

When the University of Nebraska opened their doors to higher education on September 7, 1871, joining the five faculty members were an enrollment of five freshmen (including one woman), two sophomores, and one junior. In addition to these students, there were twelve part-time students and 110 students in the University's preparatory school. According to the *Nebraska Alumnus Magazine*, "Students lived with Lincoln families, the University having decided against the 'Dormitory System.' Board and room could be obtained for $3.50 to $5 a week." Also reported: "Tuition was free to Nebraska residents, but an entrance fee of $5 was charged. Books were furnished to students at cost."

As a new University in a relatively new city, the University of Nebraska attracted talented administrative leaders and educators from eastern universities who were looking for career opportunities. By now the eastern schools were firmly established, and the University of Nebraska leadership looked eastward for guidance and inspiration in developing a high-level institution not only in academics but in competitive sports.

As the University grew, it became clear to the professors that student spirit was important to the cohesion of a college. What is school spirit and why is it important? These questions have been contemplated at the University of Nebraska since it was established. According to Robert Manley in his book, *Centennial History of the University of Nebraska,* "School spirit—the dying-for-old-Rutgers, for-God-for-country-and-for-Yale kind of alma mater-love associated with the Ivy League schools—was not notably present in the early days of the University, but as time went by more attention was given to the development of what was felt to be an essential ingredient of college life."

The faculty and administrators recognized that school spirit created identity, involvement, and loyalty among the students. The question was how to define this spirit, how to generate it, and how to maintain it, so students would be connected to the school for the success of the University. Student involvement with college athletic events and contests proved to be the key.

School spirit made a considerable advancement when a new sport called football was introduced on campus. Once football began in the college ranks, it instantly became a popular and competitive sport and spread from the East Coast westward. The early years of football at the University of Nebraska are well documented in the many books written about the Big Red. However, missing in these stories is the connection of football to school spirit and the creation of cheerleading. Given their joint advent, the history of football is interwoven with the history of college school spirit and cheerleading, and this book attempts to show how cheerleading and school spirit—discussed extensively in the previous chapter—evolved together with athletics and both grew as strongly as stalks of corn in the Cornhusker state.

Cheering fans are a natural component of being at a stadium and witnessing an exciting football game. University professors and football coaches recognized how organized cheering affected the outcome of a game. On October 10, 1902, football head coach Booth stated, "The team had more spirit than ever before, and the men would win games when they knew that the University was behind them. What is needed is more organized rooting. Those who were not in the game could not realize what a help good rooting was. The men in the bleachers could aid in winning games if they would get out and cheer at the proper times."

The efforts brought by unified yelling to help boost and motivate the team to victory helped result in successful games. The coaches recognized the impact of cheering and were eager not only to maintain it, but to increase the efforts. On

October 23, 1903, an article in *The Daily Nebraskan* reported on a football rally. One of the speakers was Professor Roscoe Pound who gave a rousing speech on rooting. In his speech he said he considered the rooters as important for the success of the game as the actual players. The realization of the impact organized cheers led by cheerleaders had on the game created an instant need, and thus game days were strategically planned and orchestrated to increase the cheers in the stands.

An article in the *Daily Nebraskan* from March 1, 1912, declared, "Rooting is not only an established but an essential part of the great American game of football. The enthusiasm of an excited, loyal crowd is contagious. And the team is susceptible to infection there from. When the team is tired, sweaty, and heart sore, when it seems they cannot keep up the fight any longer, there comes crashing out over the field a thunderous 'U-U-UNI' and the blood leaps faster through the players' veins. They grit their teeth and fight harder than ever. But in order to supply this vital stimulus those who essay to root must yell, yell, yell, without ceasing from the first kickoff to the last whistle."

"ANY FOOL CAN PLAY IT"

Prior to the beginning of football, baseball was an athletic event and the University's first intercollegiate sport. A University Baseball Association was started on October 2, 1883, with eighteen charter members and, two days later, adopted a constitution and by-laws. With the Baseball Association organized, the University Baseball Club was founded in 1884, playing their first season in the spring of 1885. Even before the organization of the Baseball Association, Nebraska challenged Doane College to a football game, but Doane refused because they were in favor of a baseball game. The baseball game with Doane took place May 15, 1882, with Doane defeating the University of Nebraska, 32 to 10. The baseball team's schedule was sporadic in the early years, playing some intercollegiate games, but mostly local teams.

As the University Baseball Club organized, so did the University of Nebraska Bicycle Club, which formed on May 20, 1884. Even though baseball was Nebraska's first sport, at the time bicycling was the most followed sport. Later, the club changed its name to the University Wheel Club and became more organized on October 10, 1891, when they adopted a constitution, elected officers, ordered uniforms, and charged charter members fifty cents to join. Eugene Brown was named captain of the University Wheel Club.

Nebraska's first baseball team, 1885. (Back row, from left) Joe Mallileau, T. S. Allen, Harry Hicks, M. I. Bigelow, W. S. Scott; (Front row, from left) C. W. Bigelow, W. F. Stephens, M. A. Whistler, T. A. Williams.

Football made its first appearance on the University of Nebraska campus during the academic year of 1882–1883, when male students were spotted kicking the ball around. When football was introduced, it changed the landscape of competitive college sports. Prior to the first game played at the University of Nebraska, very few people in the Midwest had heard of the game of football or even knew how it was played. A few University students had heard about the game being played at Harvard and Yale and tried to play, but they didn't know enough about the game to play it properly. Once football was introduced, the students kept their eyes eastward, watching the progress of the sport in eastern colleges.

The University's *Sombrero* yearbook (later the name of the yearbook was changed to the *Cornhusker*) stated this about the beginning of football on campus: "Among the most popular of athletic sports in the great dispensary of knowledge is foot-ball. This is popular for several reasons. One is that any fool can play it. Now, it takes a scientist, according to Spaulding, to play baseball; but all a man has got to have to make a successful foot-ballist is plenty of feet. Another reason of its being popular is because it is so healthful."

A member of the first football team in 1890, A. M. Troyer, reminisced on sports and football at the time he arrived on campus in 1886. He recalled that baseball was the leading game in his day. More interest was brought to the game of football when several new male students had transferred to the University from other prep schools wanting to play football. To organize a game, they all chipped in a quarter to buy a ball. A real game was not played that year, because it was a novelty just to kick the ball around. The football players would every so often choose up teams to kick the ball, with the object of playing to cross the goal line.

The next year, 1887, football continued much the same as the prior year. According to Troyer, by 1889, "Everybody seemed to have the kicking fever… even the girls looked wistfully on, and it is even rumored that they organized an eleven and practiced in the Armory behind closed doors." That same year, grounds were cleared on the northwest side of campus for a football field—known today as the legendary Memorial Stadium and site of the third largest city in Nebraska on game day Saturdays.

Interest in football was piqued on November 1, 1889, when the University of South Dakota challenged Nebraska to a football game, but the game did not materialize because Nebraska did not have a varsity football team. After the challenge was made, *The Hesperian* had this to say: "We are challenged. If there is any enthusiasm for united athletics now is the time to show it. Many individuals have been spoken to and all seem in favor of organizing a team. But here the matter sticks. No one takes hold in an energetic manner to push the organization to a completion. We have the material, the football, the grounds. All we lack is the organization and the technical knowledge. Let us put the thing through."

If college athletics were to take hold and be successful, teams had to become organized. The University of Nebraska was a leader in the West in organizing intercollegiate play. Forming a University Athletic Association was first mentioned in 1889, which was to introduce organized sports and athletics on campus. A football team needed substantial backing to become organized, but there were concerns that the athletic association did not have enough power to make this happen—for example, by enforcing the collection of dues—and they only held two to three meetings a year. *The Hesperian* noted, "The association should have the direction of all athletic affairs, the formation of college teams in the various sports, the laying out of grounds, etc."

Once again it was reported on December 2, 1889, a challenge was issued by the University of South Dakota to play Nebraska in Lincoln, and the Nebraska football committee accepted. In preparation for a football match up, the students began to arrange interclass games between the classes, to find the best athletes to form a varsity team.

A Season of Firsts

The first organized game of football played on the University of Nebraska campus was on November 23, 1889, between the senior and sophomore classes. The seniors took the honor of beating the sophomores by a score of 10 to 4. The second interclass game of football took place on December 7, 1889, between the seniors and the freshmen, with the freshmen being victorious over the seniors by a score of 6 to 4.

Students played football for fun before it became an official sport. Before the first game in 1890, an athletic association was set up for football (and for each individual sport on campus). Any student could pay a fee and join. The students would play each other on teams and then pick the best players for the varsity team.

The second challenge issued by the University of South Dakota still had not materialized by May 2, 1890. The University of South Dakota was unable to secure a workable rate for transportation for their team to afford the trip to Lincoln. The delays bought time for Nebraska's Athletic Association to become more organized before the first football game ever kicked off.

The University of Nebraska would now have an athletic association organized for each individual sport on campus. All male students were encouraged to join and pay an annual fee for membership. Contests were held with individual and interclass play to determine the best athletes in each sport. Nebraska took the lead setting up interstate contests between universities, schools, and organizations (for example, the YMCA), setting a precedent for other western universities to encourage organization of intercollegiate play. The University believed intercollegiate athletics helped the students by strengthening their bodies, which contributed to their minds and educational pursuits. Intercollegiate sports had health benefits, but it was also found to be a bonding experience for students and created a needed spirit to tie the students to their University.

The association believed, "Nothing enlivens a college so much as a body of sport-loving students." The efforts by Nebraska in organizing intercollegiate play paid off on December 28, 1891, when the Western Athletic Association was formed with Missouri, Kansas, Iowa, and Nebraska as the members.

The University of Nebraska varsity football team would be ready when the next football game challenge was presented on November 15, 1890, by the Omaha YMCA. In the fall of 1890, the University of Nebraska varsity team was organized and had ordered their uniforms; now they needed to practice. However, prior to their first intercollegiate game played on Thanksgiving Day 1890, the University of Nebraska varsity players still lacked knowledge of the fundamentals of the game of football.

A hero arrived in the form of a new faculty member, Dr. Langdon Frothingham. The University of Nebraska was able to attract top-level professors like Frothingham because the University was regarded as one of the finest academic schools in the West. Frothingham left Harvard to teach agriculture and bacteriology, and study and research veterinary medicine at the University of Nebraska. His arrival was timely in 1890, just prior to the first football down to be played at Nebraska.

Football was already firmly established at Harvard and there was already a fierce rivalry between Harvard and Yale. Frothingham brought his experience from Harvard to the students at Nebraska. Also, at the same time, Roscoe Pound, a Nebraska native, was just returning to the University of Nebraska as a student, after a year of study at Harvard. Pound returned to Nebraska full of enthusiasm after witnessing the Harvard football season of 1889.

According to historian Manley, "Pound was amused and amazed to find on his home campus 'some two dozen men, in their shirt sleeves, some in overalls, but most in their every-day trousers, and all wearing suspenders, endeavoring to learn the elements of football by the light of nature and their recollection of what they saw the year before.'"

As a returning student, Pound became the promoter of football while Frothingham provided the technical advice for the game. According to author James E. Sherwood, "By 1890 the University enrolled about five hundred students and was ready for some competition." Sherwood was an assistant professor of history at the University in 1987 when he wrote *Nebraska Football: The Coaches, the Players, the Experience*.

The students approached Frothingham to help them play football, and he was willing to assist, gathering a group of students together to explain the principles of football and organizing practice games. He promptly became the University's first coach, a volunteer position for the science professor, but he was eager to help and support the game. He knew the game of football and brought a football with him to Nebraska, so Frothingham was a natural selection as a coach. (The University didn't hire and pay a college football coach until 1893.)

Preparing for the first football game to be played, a team member, Ebenezer E. Mockett, a halfback on the team, was elected as the first captain. Mockett later recalled, "Nothing would have come of our desire to play football if Dr. Frothingham hadn't joined the faculty." Mockett was not only a great football player but an all-around excellent athlete, including being an award-winning bicyclist. Mockett entered his first bicycle race in Omaha on September 19, 1890, and went on to win races and break records all over the United States. He rode a big front-wheel cycle 219.8 miles in twelve hours, which won him the state championship. Mockett received over one hundred trophies, medals, and awards during his athletic career.

Walt Dobbins, a sports writer for the *Evening Journal*, called Mockett "one of the greatest living athletes in the country." His honors were won in lacrosse, bowling, bicycling, roller skating, ice skating, and football, and he was the captain of each team and/or champion of each event. In the 1890s, while Mockett was captain of the football team, he claimed bicycling was his favorite sport. After college he served as an exhibition rider for bicycle manufacturers and as a salesman and later a purchasing agent for the Fowler Cycle Works of Chicago.

After his career in cycling, Mockett settled back in Lincoln and owned a car dealership. He remained a lifelong sports enthusiast. Through the years, Mockett continued being a football fan of the Cornhuskers, attending the Rose Bowl of 1940. For his athletic efforts in football, he received a lifetime free pass, stamped with the number eighty-four, to all Cornhusker home football games. The pass should have been number one, but he didn't hear about the passes until fifteen years after he graduated from the University. Mockett would later state that his key to athletic success was to "go to bed early every night and don't drink."

The first competitive football game of the University of Nebraska was played on November 27, 1890, in Omaha. *The Hesperian* knew the team needed support and urged the brass band and yell squad (not a formal organization yet) to attend the first away game. The University's military band also attended the first game and provided musical entertainment from the sidelines.

Nebraska's team called themselves the Old Gold Knights and wore canvas outfits they called uniforms. According to a book by three editors at the *Omaha World-Herald*, the uniforms resembled a "flour sack." (Howard Silber, James Denney, and Hollis Limprecht were in the editorial department at the paper, and their 1966 book was titled *Go Big Red*.) The faculty reached into their pockets and donated the funds for the white canvas uniforms with black stockings, at a total cost of $35. Even though the school color was gold, later the players sported red stockings, a sign of colors to come.

Nebraska's first football team played their first game on Thanksgiving Day, 1890. In their canvas uniforms (front row, from left), E. Girard, quarter; Coach Langdon Frothingham; Harry Lord, sub for quarter; Morrow, fullback; Charles Stroman, sub; J. H. Johnston, right back; (back row, from left) C. M. Skiles, right end; Captain Ebenezer E. Mockett, left back; Charles D. Chandler, left tackle; Fred Hyde, right guard; A. M. Anderson, snapback; Stockton, left guard; J. C. Porterfield, right tackle, and L. E. Troyer, left end rusher.

A First Game Win: 10-0

According to *The Hesperian*, the first season the varsity football players provided the cost of their train fare to the games. They boarded the train with at least forty fans bound for Omaha to witness the first game that Thanksgiving Day in 1890. During the train trip the fans refrained from yelling as to not disturb the other passengers, but revelers could no longer contain themselves upon their arrival. As the train pulled into Omaha's Union Station, a thunderous University yell was carried out, and "Omaha was apprised of our arrival."

The University of Nebraska won their first game 10 to 0. After the game, as the University of Nebraska fans left the grandstands at the Omaha YMCA, the opposing fans "parted in order to make room for our long and continuous cheering, our repeated yells and exclamations. While the air was still vibrating from the yell and while echoes were coming back, we left the ball park with flying colors."

On the train ride home, the fans filled the air with yells and songs, which entertained some of the other passengers and caused others to flee to neighboring train cars. It was reported, "Pound, '88, was the most enthusiastic man of our party. He originated the flag scheme, and covered himself with glory, by composing the classical songs by which we entertained the common people on the way home from Omaha and persisted in singing until we had a whole coach to ourselves."

The account goes on: "From the fertile brain of Pound emanated the quite classical song: *'Frigida dies est cum relinquimur, est cum relinquimur, est cum relinquimur; Frigida dies, est cum relinquimur.'*" The songs continued with Pound's other Latin selection, "*Cum diptulis dersalibus non affecti, non affecti, non affecti sumus. Ad infinitum.*" [The songs are translated in a later chapter.]

Once the exuberant fans returned to Lincoln, they were met at the train platform by a crowd of University students. The crowd greeted them with yells and songs, as they continued to celebrate Nebraska's first football game and victory. As the evening was winding down, "the enthusiastic party was broken up; and each one went home to dream sweet dreams of foot-ball at Omaha."

Since the first intercollegiate game of football against Omaha in 1890, the loyal fans have turned out at home games and followed the team to away games, lending their voices and support.

The second and final game of the season was after the new year on February 3, 1891, against Doane College. The University's varsity team rode the train to the town of Crete along with fifty students. There was silence on the train in anticipation of saving their voices for the game. Roscoe Pound rode the train and handed out canes and hats decorated in the "old gold" school colors.

When the train arrived, Doane students and even several members of the Doane football team came to meet the Nebraska team and fans at the station. Having held practice on a muddy field, the Doane players were covered in mud—surely putting fear in the heart of the opposing fans.

In the grandstands to watch the game were more Doane fans than Nebraska fans, but the Nebraska fans were more vocal and enthusiastic. After the game, on the train ride home, the fans celebrated their 18 to 0 victory over Doane by singing Pound's Latin songs. Once again, upon the train's return to Lincoln, the band and a crowd of students were awaiting their arrival. The students formed an impromptu parade headed by the band and carried their celebration through town, finally disbanding around one o'clock in the morning.

After two away games, the first football season had come to an end. Pound recounted the first football season of 1890: "Some of the men who played that year had not a little natural ability and would have done well in time with proper training. Dr. Frothingham, who had seen the best of football, did what he could for them, and as opposing teams were equally raw, individual strength and athletic skill took our first varsity team triumphantly through its first season."

A game played in 1913 against Minnesota, with Nebraska cheerleader in foreground wearing white.

The season had ended and Frothingham resigned from the University faculty to return to Harvard to accept a position with the medical school. But even without their heroic coach, the football team had forged a winning tradition, and the excitement of football at the University of Nebraska had begun.

The Nebraska football program continued to build. During the fall of 1892, the training table was introduced. *The Hesperian* reported, "A 'training table' has been started and now the football player will have only such a diet as will build up and give endurance. Such a move can only result in good."

ADMISSION TO HOME GAMES: 25 CENTS

During the first year of football at Nebraska, the fans were not charged an admission fee. By the second year the crowds had steadily grown, and the athletic department decided to charge twenty-five cents a game—a sum that did not deter the fans who were now interested in supporting the game. The students wanted a home game, and the first one took place on October 31, 1891, against Doane College at the Nebraska home field of Lincoln Park, in Lincoln, Nebraska. The first home game resulted in a win for Nebraska over Doane, 28 to 4.

Along with the increased interest in football games came an increase in admission prices. On September 19, 1902, prior to the fall football season, student season tickets sold for $2.50 for seven games. On January 9, 1902, *The Daily Nebraskan* reported on the cost of football for the previous 1901 season:

Supplies, outfitting, medical care, etc.	$786.55
Coach	$600.00
Postage, printing, advertising	$90.65
Care of grounds	$44.83
Training table	$468.52
Travel expense	$1,127.49
Miscellaneous expense	$94.60
Permanent improvements	$1,677.48
Total	**$4,890.12**

With total expenses for the 1901 football season at almost $5,000, that's a sharp contrast to the business of football today, which for the 2015–2016 school year, Nebraska athletics generated over $112 million in revenue and paid more than $103 million in expenses. Of course, the cost of a season ticket has increased somewhat, if you can even get your hands on reserved seats today.

On September 18, 1902, an article appeared in *The Daily Nebraskan* by an unknown author giving advice to potential football players on what it means and what it takes to be a University of Nebraska player:

> *Your "spirit" will be one of the chief points considered in selecting men for the varsity squad. No matter how much knowledge of the game you may have or how experienced you may be, your value will depend chiefly on your willingness to subordinate yourself to coach and captain and make your interests secondary to those of the team. Don't play football for a sweater, for the trips which you make with the team, for free admission to all games.*

Play because you love to play, because you want the drill and the discipline which comes with it and because you are proud to represent Nebraska on victorious fields.

The popularity of football steadily increased with a noticeable boost in school spirit, contributed by several winning seasons, and organized cheerleading was well under way. The students and sports fans, since the 1890s, had been focused on winning no matter the contest, but there began an air of change in what really mattered. A boost in school spirit was being felt and was best described in a story from the 1909 *Cornhusker* yearbook about football, recounting when school spirit made an impact on campus:

ON A LATE October morning of the season of 1904 the railroad station was thronged with students of the University of Nebraska. That sober autumnal morning was enlivened by waiving [sic] streamers and pennants of scarlet and cream, rousing Cornhusker yells and songs to old Nebraska and her team. For a full hour before the arrival of the train that was bringing back our defeated football team from Minnesota, that great crowd of rooters evinced a genuine spirit of true sportsmanship. Rousing speeches were made that contained some singularly striking truths concerning college sports.

Doctor Roscoe Pound, that most amiable dean of those days, displaying as he always did a fine patriotism for his own University, impressed his hearers with the necessity of standing by the team at all times. Our own Dr. Condra spoke with splendid spirit. He reminded the men and women of Nebraska that the squad that was coming home that morning were "our boys," that they had been fighting "our battles," and that we should be with them in their defeats as well as in their victories. When at last the train pulled in the football team was borne high on the shoulders of stalwart and big-hearted men. A great bandwagon, decorated in our magnificent colors, was drawn through the streets by a thousand cheering students. Flowers were showered upon the men of the gridiron by loyal co-eds. The songs and cheers there at the homecoming of a defeated team touched a responsive chord in the hearts of all true Cornhuskers.

This was the best lesson in college spirit ever taught at Nebraska. The team had lost its biggest game, yet no squad had ever been received with such pomp and display. The spirit of good fellowship prevailed there, and it seemed at last that the people were beginning to understand the real business of football in a university.

The passion for winning games had been cooled. The notion of winning, winning at any cost, was somehow superseded by a sense of love and respect for the squad of men who had journeyed so far to fight a battle which was not indeed, the squad's battle, but which was in every sense the affair of the whole school. We who were there that morning seemed to appreciate the feelings of the men who had endured the exacting discipline of a season's training....We cheered and yelled ourselves hoarse over a beaten team and, what was best of all, we were beginning to understand the spirit that prompted us to do it.

Racism and One of Nebraska's Greatest Athletes

The University of Nebraska began proving to be a progressive school both on and off the field. For instance, an important first for University of Nebraska athletics was a football player by the name of George Flippin who was the first African American athlete at Nebraska and quickly became the University's first football star. Flippin was a ruggedly handsome student standing at 6 feet 2 inches, 200 pounds, who played tackle, running back, and fullback for the football team. He played on the team from 1891 to 1894, earning three varsity letters. Also, during these four years, Flippin was one of only five African American athletes in the college ranks of the entire nation.

George Flippin was a versatile athlete. Not only was he a football star, but he was also a wrestler, track and field athlete, and a baseball player. During the football season, prior to a scheduled match between Nebraska and Missouri, the University of Missouri informed Nebraska they would not play the game if Flippin was on the team. Thus, the first Nebraska vs. Missouri game ended in a Nebraska win by forfeit. According to author Kathy Nelson, "Years later, Flippin would joke that he beat Missouri single-handedly."

A positive outcome from the Missouri incident occurred prior to the start of the 1893 season. The governing committee of the Interstate University Athletic Association made a decision in light of Missouri's forfeiture of the game with Nebraska to institute a new rule to levy a fine of $50 on a school for refusal to play an opponent. The fee was a hefty sum considering a typical entrance fee charged for admission to a game was twenty-five cents.

George Flippin, Nebraska's first African American football player and star athlete, 1894.

The Missouri incident was not an isolated event of racism facing Flippin while on the team. Another incident occurred during the same season, after a game in Denver with Nebraska playing the Denver Athletic Club. After the game, the Nebraska team planned to attend a play at the Denver Opera House following a dinner at the Brown Palace Hotel, but the evening was cut short when the management of both businesses refused entrance to Flippin. In support of their teammate, the Nebraska football team decided to retire early for the evening. Not only did Flippin endure racism off the field, but on the field opponents would slug and kick him. The courage he displayed in the face of such treatment garnered the respect of his teammates.

When the next season arrived, George Flippin was unanimously elected as team captain by his teammates. However, not everyone associated with the

Nebraska football team with George Flippin (second row, third from left) and his teammates, 1892.

team was supportive of Flippin being named team captain. Nebraska's first official paid coach, Frank Crawford, stated, "It takes a man with brains to be a captain; all there is to Flippin is brute force. He is slow in getting signals. He can't play a fast game."

After leaving the University of Nebraska, Flippin, defying Crawford's assertion, went on to be awarded a medical degree in 1900 from the University of Illinois College of Physicians and Surgeons, following in his physician parents' footsteps. After medical school, Flippin opened a medical practice and the first hospital named Mawood, in Stromsburg, Nebraska.

Flippin was a bright man who knew his civil rights. He was not timid about standing up for himself, his civil rights, and his beliefs and fighting racial adversity throughout his life. Flippin died in 1929, and representatives of the University of Nebraska Letterman's Club were in attendance at his funeral. Flippin was inducted into the Nebraska Football Hall of Fame forty-five years following his death and holds the honor as the first black football player to be admitted. Also, as recently as November 2015, the *Omaha World-Herald* published its list of Nebraska's 100 greatest athletes, and George Flippin was ranked number ninety-eight.

Flippin was immortalized in 2006 on the Guardians of the Gate— the doors that open to the legendary Tunnel Walk into Memorial Stadium. As reported by Randy York of Randy's N-Sider Column, Joe Putjenter of Omaha had this to say about George Flippin:

> *When I was first asked to design Memorial Stadium's Tunnel Walk gates, I did a lot of research on the history on Nebraska football. I was in search of a way to represent guardians of Nebraska football history. My idea was that every time the players ran on the field they were passing through history and making history. The idea I wanted was all Bugeaters, with George Flippin in the middle (as he is now). My final design had Husker legends drawn in an art deco style, so we could tie into the style of the State Capitol Building. Even though that idea didn't get approved, I liked the design and story behind the Flippin-led Bugeaters. I love George Flippin's story of hard work and perseverance. I thought it represented Nebraska football well. In my opinion, George Flippin should be as well known as any of our current stars, including Heisman Trophy winners Johnny Rodgers, Eric Crouch, and Mike Rozier. I think George Flippin holds up as a role model. His place on the Tunnel Walk gates is a fitting tribute, but his story of fighting racism and prejudice and succeeding against all odds is a story that every Husker fan, Husker player, and Husker recruit should know.*

The Guardians of the Gate are protected by members of the armed services prior to the home game Tunnel Walk. The bronze and glass gates depict former Husker legends Bob Brown, George Sauer, George Flippin, Guy Chamberlin, Sam Francis, and Bob Reynolds. The first servicemen to protect the gates were Sergeant Michael Sharples and Specialist Richard Delancey, both Bronze Star recipients for valor of the Nebraska National Guard.

At moments in time, the University of Nebraska was progressive and a leader in equality and desegregation of college sports and cheerleading. Then again, at later times other standout African American athletes who followed Flippin were prohibited from playing on teams at the University.

According to Husker historian Mike Babcock, "After 1917, blacks were no longer allowed to enroll in graduate school at Nebraska, and they were prevented from competing in varsity athletics and participating in the band. There would be no black Cornhusker athletes again until the early 1950s." Shortly thereafter, Nebraska's first African American cheerleader, Annette Hudson, graced the Yell Squad in 1969, creating another first in Nebraska sports history.

The early success of the football team created an explosion of interest in sports on campus for both men and women and created another first for women. In the late 1890s, Victorian values were loosening their grip, and women experienced a newfound freedom to explore physical activity. University of Nebraska women literally took the ball and ran with it, creating the first women's basketball team in 1896, which led to the beginning of intercollegiate sports for women when the basketball team played Council Bluffs in 1898. Also, in 1917, women students were coming to the forefront to make history in cheerleading at the University of Nebraska and for the first time nationally on college campuses.

Annette Hudson (front row, second from left) was Nebraska Yell Squad's first African American member, 1969 to 1972. The Yell Squad posed for this November 21, 1970, football program cover for the Oklahoma vs. Nebraska football game.

THE BIRTH OF THE HUSKER NATION

The introduction of HuskerVision changed fan engagement in Memorial Stadium. The University of Nebraska was a leader in big screen, instant replays in the stadium, and was the first college to bring this experience to the fans. A former University of Nebraska graduate, Jeff Schmahl, in 1993, left his career as a sports anchor in Lincoln to create HuskerVision for the University. It took some convincing for the University to see Schmahl's vision of the future and impact of video broadcasting to a big screen and how it would change the fan experience. In 1994, HuskerVision was born, and after that came the creation of the now famous, spine-tingling Husker's Tunnel Walk as we know it today. Schmahl is recognized as the Father of HuskerVision.

The importance of the support and interaction of the cheering fans and players is witnessed today in the Tunnel Walk—a ritual prior to every home game. The Tunnel Walk tradition began in 1994, from the southwest corner of the stadium. Since 2006, the players emerge from their new locker rooms in the northwest corner to begin the Tunnel Walk through a maze of cheering Cornhusker fans. The players are led in the Tunnel Walk parade by their head coach and, in turn, touch the lucky horseshoe above the exit of the north stadium. The lucky horseshoe has followed the change in locker rooms and used to hang above the entrance in the original north stadium, before the Tom and Nancy Osborne Athletic Complex was added.

Once the players are blessed by touching the lucky horseshoe, they step on a specially designed Astroturf known as the Big Red Carpet. The Tunnel Walk's red carpet is lined with cheering Husker fans whose adoration is designed to energize the team, and that energy intensifies as the team approaches the field. HuskerVision films the Tunnel Walk and projects the video onto the massive Jumbotrons in the stadium so the fans in the stadium may share in the excitement of the approaching Husker players as they make their way through the tunnel. The players burst onto the field—running as the Yell Squad and Spirit Squad lead the way—as the stadium rocks to the rousing rally of the Alan Parsons Project's "Sirius." The pregame pageantry on the field then begins.

The early years started with humble beginnings and grew to today's pageantry, and has created a bond, a connection, between the individual player and the team, and this bond extends to the fans. This bond is described by Roscoe Pound, when in 1893, Pound quoted the author of *Tom Brown* as stating this about the connection: "The discipline and reliance on one another which it teaches is so valuable—it ought to be such an unselfish game. It merges the individual in the eleven, he doesn't play that he may win, but that his side may." Pound also said, "And we are thankful that we may at least come out and cheer for you as you win her renown—a renown all her children rejoice in, since being hers it belongs to all of us."

From the beginning, football, school spirit, and cheerleading have gone hand-in-hand in making game day a complete experience, and this will continue to be true into the future.

In 1905, John Rice, student and literary editor of *The Daily Nebraskan*, described this connection:

> *Wearing representative colors, the team lines up against the players of a rival institution, imbued with the same sense of loyalty and ambition to win as themselves. It is then that the student feels the thrill of personal interest and lends his voice to the singing of songs and to the clamor of inspiring yells. Fully awakened, it is his sense of loyalty to his institution and its interests that is finding a vent. Can it, then, be denied that football serves to create a devotion and loyalty among the students for their college? The impressions are lasting and the graduate going forth upon the world's highway carries them with him. The conclusion can readily be drawn that just as a united and loyal people make a nation strong, just so does a united, loyal, and active student body give strength to its institution.*

As so aptly described in 1905, the united and loyal people that make a strong nation are today called Husker Nation.

4

THE EVER-LASTING INFLUENCE OF ROSCOE AND LOUISE POUND

Buildings named Pound Hall can be found on two college campuses in the United States—one at the University of Nebraska–Lincoln and one at Harvard University. The existence of two Pound Halls is a fitting tribute to the extraordinary lives, amazing achievements, and lifetime of competition between the brother and sister Nebraskans named Pound.

In the years since its construction in 1969, Pound Hall was a residential dormitory on the campus of the University of Nebraska. But I must tell you there is more to the name than just a mortar-and-glass building. Pound Hall was dedicated to Dr. Louise Pound to honor a career of devotion to students and her astounding accomplishments as an English professor at the University. On December 22, 2017, due to age and costs to renovate, Pound Hall and its adjoining Cather Hall were demolished. University Suites and Eastside Suites were built to replace the student housing needs. The Willa Cather Dining Complex was built to replace the Cather-Pound Dining Center.

The site of the original Pound Hall has been turned into green space, with no plans for construction on the site. But in June 2018, the University of Nebraska Board of Regents approved renaming the longtime College of Business Administration (CBA) building located on campus as Louise Pound Hall. The renaming was made possible by the unveiling in 2018 of the new $84 million College of Business Administration building. The old CBA building, then, has been repurposed and renamed to continue to honor

Renaming of the CBA building to Louise Pound Hall, June 2018.

Louise Pound for her scholarly and athletic contribution to the University of Nebraska, as well as for the equal opportunities she created for female students during her fifty-year career.

The second Pound Hall is located on the campus of Harvard University in honor of the distinguished career of Louise's brother, Dr. Roscoe Pound, the dean of Harvard Law School from 1916 to 1936.

To understand the profound influence of the Pound family on Nebraska school spirit and women's role in athletics—an impact so significant that buildings were named after them—we must return to the late 1800s and look more closely into the Pound family history.

THE POUND FAMILY BECOMES THE UNIVERSITY'S BIGGEST CHEERLEADERS

West of the Missouri River lay the vast, undisturbed Great Plains. The Territory of Nebraska and in particular Lincoln, as a new city, was a blank slate—a flat prairie without a tree or bush in sight. The territory was still unsettled and populated by wild animals and Native Americans. However, the 1860 census counted 28,841 persons living in Nebraska striving to make a new life, most by living off the land. The capital of the Nebraska Territory was originally located in Omaha but changed to Lincoln in 1867. The capital move was a result of issues brought on by political wrangling, bolstered by the potential monetary value in a salt basin and a consideration of the ideal location where the new University was to be built. Even though the salt basin later proved not to be a profitable venture, the legislature voted in favor of moving the capital and locating the new University in Lincoln.

At the time Lincoln was named the state's capital city, the population of the city was fewer than thirty people, the city's development was still in the early stages, and few roads were paved. By the time the University opened its doors four years later, the population had grown to 2,000 residents.

The Board of Regents initially set aside four blocks of land north of the city to lay out the University. According to Robert Knoll, an emeritus professor of English who wrote many books on Nebraska history, "Roscoe Pound said generations later that his father, Judge Stephen B. Pound, had suggested to the commissioners that four square blocks was hardly room enough for a University; but the commissioners ignored the protest, and so for the next century the University had to buy back land which ought to have been part of the initial settlement." The city of Lincoln was booming and developing by 1890, with the installation of electric lights, a water system, and the beginning of paved roads.

Roscoe and Louise's parents, Stephen and Laura Biddlecombe Pound, were both born and raised in upstate New York. As a newly married couple in February 1869, they set out to move westward to begin their new life together and to settle into the excitement of a new city and state. The potential in opportunity and possibilities attracted the young newlyweds westward to the Great Plains. The Pounds felt the city of Lincoln was the ideal place to begin a career, settle, and raise a family. Stephen and Laura had the freedom to help mold and shape the city into a progressive venue to raise their children: Roscoe, Louise, and Olivia. As the city grew and prospered, so did the University of Nebraska and the Pound family. The city was growing into a leading learning center with developing intellectual and cultural opportunities, which was an ideal fit for the Pound family.

Stephen Pound was a man known for his integrity, as he built a successful law practice in Lincoln. He has been described by his son and contemporaries who knew him as a reserved, scrupulous, and truthful gentleman. Stephen was deliberate in his actions when it came to the law, had a laid-back personality, and worked at a slower pace. In his spare time his interests were centered on following athletics, and he focused his attention on football, baseball, and boxing. As a father, he shared his interest in sports with his children and had an influence on Roscoe and Louise in developing their love of athletics.

The Pounds complemented each other, being a like-minded couple and highly intelligent. Yet in contrast to her husband, Laura was tiny and frail-looking, but this appearance belied her physical abilities; she was a boundless whirlwind of energy. As a child, Laura described herself as small for her age, but she was athletic and could outrun boys her own age. When playing with other girls in jump rope contests, Laura had the stamina to beat her friends. Prior to her marriage to Stephen, she attended college and enjoyed a career as a teacher, which accounted for the value she placed on education.

The Pound family values were based on their Quaker heritage. The Quakers believed in equal education for both boys and girls, thus the Pounds carried on these beliefs when bringing up their own children. As a young wife and mother, Laura set an example for her children by continuing to take classes in the German language and English literature at the University of Nebraska. Taking additional classes at the University helped ensure she would be prepared to be the best teacher for her children, who were homeschooled. Laura followed the example set by her own mother, Olivia, who homeschooled Laura and her siblings. Laura's decision to educate at home went against conventional thinking for educating children at the time, but that did not deter her.

In Lincoln, eyebrows were raised when Laura installed a blackboard on the living room wall of her home. Pound biographer Marie Krohn stated, "Hanging a blackboard in the room reserved for entertaining guests was a daring act for a woman of Laura's time and place. As the wife of a lawyer, who aimed to establish a trustworthy and respected practice, she was expected to create a formal home atmosphere, one that banished children and their belongings to unseen parts of the house. Instead of following customs of the day, Laura decided to carry out her own ideas about raising and educating children."

Marie Krohn is the admired author of several books. Most notably, she wrote the 2007 biography, *Louise Pound: The 19th Century Iconoclast Who Forever Changed America's Views about Women, Academics, and Sports.*

Equal opportunity was ingrained early in the lives of the Pound children. Laura encouraged and influenced her daughters to reject the conventional female roles of the current Victorian era. An experience during Laura's childhood had an impact on her after witnessing her father voting while her mother was forced to stay home. Going forward, Laura Pound always supported women's suffrage for the right to vote—a cause Louise later championed.

Krohn reported, "When deciding how to educate their children, Stephen and Laura Pound disregarded prevailing beliefs. They ignored education tracts, advising parents to avoid taxing their daughters' brains with masculine subjects such as science and mathematics. Other advice they refused to follow came from physicians, who warned that playing sports might damage girls' reproductive organs. Both parents considered their daughters capable of learning the same subjects as Roscoe, and they never discouraged Louise and Olivia from playing outdoor games."

A competitive nature developed among the siblings, particularly between Roscoe and Louise, and was encouraged by their parents. The siblings enjoyed friendly rivalries with each other. "Laura Pound encouraged the cooperative spirit between her children as she supervised their play and educated them at home," according to Krohn. As the younger sister, Louise was motivated by wanting to keep up with her older brother and compete with him. Roscoe invited Louise to play in games with him and his friends, so she grew up feeling equal. Krohn said, "She doesn't tag along behind her brother, but races beside him as they run across fields or read books together."

The Pound children were all exceptionally intelligent and that intellect was nourished by both their parents. Because Stephen was a prominent lawyer, the Pounds were an influential couple who were rising in the social circles of Lincoln. The Pounds regularly entertained dignitaries and faculty members in their home. The children were not dismissed from the adult conversations, and they felt accepted and welcomed as peers in adult-level discussions. The exposure gave the Pound children an acceptance and confidence around adults.

Krohn wrote, "Mingling with influential Lincolnites allowed the children to develop a confident ease of manner in official situations. Louise and Roscoe, especially, never hesitated to question authority." This characteristic would later prove a necessity for Louise as she fought for opportunities for female students at the University.

When the Pound children's homeschooling ended, they enrolled in the University's preparatory school and took classes in German and beginning Latin. Later as University students, the intellectual environment continued to enrich their minds, and in return, the Pounds enriched the University and the lives of the students.

The Pound family is intimately related to the early years of Lincoln and to the University of Nebraska in the areas of education, law, athletics, equal rights, and cheerleading. All three of the Pound children attended the University of Nebraska. Roscoe, Louise, and Olivia dedicated their lives to their careers of education and scholarly pursuits. Roscoe was the only one to marry but did not have children, so the Pound family line ended with the brilliant siblings. Both Roscoe and Louise had illustrious careers at the University, contributing ideas, innovations, leadership, and influence.

In the Pounds' commitment to the University, they considered the institution and students a part of their family and, thus, felt a personal ownership in the University of Nebraska. The next sections explore their contributions in more detail—especially as the Pounds evolved into Nebraska's biggest cheerleaders.

Roscoe Pound—Great Legal Mind and Die-Hard Football Fan

Nathan Roscoe Pound (1870–1964) was known as Roscoe throughout his lifetime. Roscoe was a child prodigy with a photographic memory. According to W. W. Ray in a research paper, "At an early age he astounded others by his capacity to rattle off long passages after scanning the text but once." Pound could speed read and knew several languages including Greek, Latin, German, Hebrew, Sanskrit, French, Italian, and a bit of Russian.

He was born in Lincoln, Nebraska, on October 27, 1870, to parents who passed on to their son their passion for learning and a love of athletics. His parents encouraged him in both his academic and physical pursuits. Pound was initially enrolled in the public school system in Lincoln, but this soon ended when school proved too slow and he was easily bored, which led him to cause mischief. He was high spirited and a bit of a prankster. Even as an adult he was known to enjoy a good prank. In order to keep him challenged and his education on track, his mother took it upon herself to educate him at home.

In 1882, he was ready for the next phase of his education, and at the age of twelve he entered Latin school, a preparatory department at the University of Nebraska.

At the University he developed an interest in military science and joined the cadets, rising to the rank of captain. The military cadets drilled, marched, played musical instruments and were the beginning of what would later become the University Marching Band. The band's first official appearance occurred when the military cadet band performed at the University of Nebraska in April of 1880. While a military cadet, Pound memorized and mastered the art of marching and drills. He did not have a natural ability for playing a musical instrument, however, and never took up playing, even though he had a lifelong appreciation for music.

The musical talent in the Pound family was his sister Louise, whose instrument was the piano, and she would later obtain her degree in music from the University. Roscoe enjoyed listening to Louise play the piano as she entertained her family and guests in their family home. It was a natural fit for Roscoe to be a drum major, and he served in that capacity from 1882 to 1888. He used his familiarity of the military band to recruit their services to add spirit and enthusiasm to the game of football beginning with the first game in 1890.

Pound earned three degrees in botany, all at the University of Nebraska. In 1888, when Pound received his BA, his father wasn't sure how his son could use his botany degree in the real world and felt it was impractical. However, botany was still Pound's first love, and he developed an interest in natural sciences, entomology, and botany, all areas which his mother encouraged during his youth. The summer after he achieved his degree, Pound studied the law with his father, attending lectures on law and completing two evening law courses, which pleased his father immensely.

In 1888, when classes resumed in the fall, Pound enrolled in graduate school to continue his work in botany and received his master's degree in 1889. Then Pound left Lincoln to study law at Harvard for a year in 1889—a move that was encouraged by his father who was a practicing lawyer in Lincoln, an elected judge, and who served in the state senate. His father saw a future for his son in the practice of law.

As a student at Harvard, Pound considered continuing his studies in botany, but during his year at Harvard Law School he began to enjoy his legal studies and made his choice to pursue law. He had been accustomed to the text-lecture method of law school as taught in Nebraska and had misgivings when he was first introduced to the casebook system at Harvard. (The casebook method—reading actual judicial opinions—is currently the primary method of teaching law in the United States.)

Pound began to shift his opinion after the first month of school when he admitted to his father that the casebook system seemed the better way to study the law. Also, while a student at Harvard, he was first exposed to the excitement of football, cheering, and school spirit. Despite his academic interest in the law, after one year of law study, Pound left Harvard to return to Lincoln in 1890 and never received his law degree. His hasty return to Lincoln was spurred by the ill health of his father and a need to help his father's law practice.

He Possessed a Good Loud Voice (In Latin, No Less)

Upon returning to Lincoln in 1890, he interned at his father's law firm. Once, while visiting with a lawyer family friend, the attorney said, "Roscoe, you know enough law now to pass the state bar. When you call on the examiner, take along a box of good cigars." Pound won over the examiner and was admitted to the state bar at the age of twenty.

What he experienced at Harvard accompanied him back to Lincoln, and he was enormously influential in the development of the fledgling sport of football at the University of Nebraska. Organizing a University team required a leader.

Pound filled that role with his football knowledge and experience from Harvard. At Nebraska, Pound was a vocal advocate and assisted in leading the campaign for a football team. With his enthusiasm for the game, he became the organizer, referee, fund-raiser, cheerleader, and anything else that was needed to get football organized and played.

In addition to his work as an organizer, Pound was one of Nebraska's first die-hard football fans. While a student, he was too small to participate in athletics, due to his young age when attending the University, but he possessed a good loud voice. His enthusiasm and vocal strength made him one of the University's best rooters and cheerleaders. He was one of the few students and professors who rode the train with the team to the first game against Omaha's YMCA in 1890. On the train he led everyone in his two Latin victory songs he wrote.

Although the words were sung in Latin, Pound's victory song is more poetic when translated:

**IT IS A COLD DAY,
WHEN WE ARE LEFT ALONE,
IT IS, WHEN WE ARE LEFT ALONE,
IT IS, WHEN WE ARE LEFT ALONE,
IT IS A COLD DAY,
WHEN WE ARE LEFT ALONE**

Or

**THE DAY IS COLD,
WHEN WE ARE LEFT BEHIND,
IT IS, WHEN WE ARE LEFT BEHIND,
IT IS, WHEN WE ARE LEFT BEHIND,
THE DAY IS COLD,
WHEN WE ARE LEFT BEHIND**

The second Latin victory song was used at the time to say: "I feel like I feel, like I feel, like I feel…" Both victory songs were examined and translated for this book by Dr. William Nethercut, in the department of classics at the University of Texas at Austin. According to Dr. Nethercut, the second song may have had this effect: "With a HEY and a HI, it's nothing to us, not a bit, not a bit. And say all this again and again and again and never stop ever."

Pound was known to be fun loving, a bit of a jokester. This side of Pound is shown in the second cheer since the Latin words "*diptulis dersalibus*" are not Latin words at all, and he is playing with his fellow rooters, with made-up words.

According to Paul Sayre, a law professor at the University of Iowa, in his 1948 book, Pound described his experience of the final contest of the season: "I saw the closing game. It was a glorious victory, and I got home from Omaha speechless and dead broke."

After another game, at Iowa, he commented on the after-effects of his own enthusiasm, by saying, "The speechlessness was acquired in the service of my country, as the subjoined clipping will indicate: Roscoe Pound, assisted by Charley Jones, was in charge of the vocal part of the game. He pressed the button and the voices did the rest. The boys cheered by sections, by platoons and then in unison. They belched all kinds of noises out of their horns and throats. They sang in all kinds of keys and they sang all kinds of songs. The firmament shook visibly several times when Mr. Pound decided that it was time for an outbreak. If Iowa was not sufficiently overcome by the violence of Nebraska's rushes, the music and the cheering were enough to complete the job."

As a practicing lawyer, Pound taught his first law class at the University of Nebraska in Roman law during the spring of 1895. Pound also continued his own studies and completed his PhD in botany in 1898. His specialty in botany was phytogeography, which is the study of the relationship of Nebraska plants to the environment. As with many firsts, Pound was the first person to receive a doctoral degree from the University of Nebraska at Lincoln.

Throughout his life he continued to pursue his interest in science and botany. As an adult it was not unusual for Pound and a colleague to go off hiking and bicycling in the remote, wide open plains of Nebraska to study, discover, and classify plants. He was founder and the first director of the Nebraska Botanical Survey. His research and discovery led to a fungus parasite being named after him and known as *Roscoepoundia*.

But he was equally captivated by his work in the law. Wigdor stated, "He was an energetic, highly motivated botanist, but he was an even busier lawyer." In 1900, Pound helped organize the Nebraska Bar Association, later becoming dean of the law college from 1903 to 1907 while concurrently teaching law at the University of Nebraska. According to Wigdor, "He was a strong-willed young man who thrived on challenging problems, and he moved effortlessly into positions of intellectual and institutional leadership."

Founding of the Innocents Society to Boost School Spirit

Pound particularly enjoyed working with and providing guidance to the male students on campus. One of his major accomplishments in organizing male students was in establishing the Innocents Society. The Innocents began as a Chancellor's Senior Honor Society of the top male students on campus, dedicated to the enhancement and leadership of the University and student body. Pound passed on his love of cheering and school spirit to the members of the Innocents Society, and once the so-called secret group was established in 1903, their number-one priority was taking over and organizing cheerleading at the University. (The Innocents Society was so instrumental in University cheerleading, details are revealed in the next chapter.)

Pound was steadfast in wanting to improve the University's College of Law and he was insistent that improvements be made to rank the college with the best in the country. In 1904, he changed the college's standards by increasing the requirements for admission, increased the length of attendance to two years, and introduced the casebook system. Under his deanship, the college reorganized, improved, and grew. Pound approached the University for more money to be applied to the College of Law to further his efforts, but he was turned down.

Roscoe Pound in a studio portrait in his later years.

Pound left Nebraska in 1907 to teach law at Northwestern University and then Chicago University. It was speculated that one reason for his departure from Nebraska was due to being turned down for the money he felt he needed to continue improving the College of Law. Students were shocked when word spread of his pending departure, and they protested and rallied on his behalf to the University leaders to retain him. The efforts were to no avail. It was time for Pound to move on in his career.

Shortly after a teaching stint at Chicago University, Pound accepted a teaching position at Harvard University in 1910. He would later become dean of the law school at Harvard from 1916 to 1936, continuing his long and illustrious career in the field of law.

Pound was a prolific writer, and, by the age of seventy, he was credited with the authorship of 773 books, speeches, and essays. Throughout his career and lifetime, Pound was known for his oration, quick wit, and humor. Upon retiring as dean of Harvard Law, he accepted a position as professor emeritus with Harvard. At the age of seventy-seven he learned the Chinese language, so he could go to China to better advise Chiang Kai-Shek, the president of the Republic of China, on legal administration and reorganization of the Chinese judiciary system.

"When asked upon his return from China how he had managed to do so well with no prior knowledge of the Chinese language, he replied that he had experienced some difficulties in the first six weeks but after that he had got along fine without an interpreter," according to W. W. Ray. Such a humble response when referring to learning one of the most difficult languages in the world further demonstrates the ease with which Pound soaked up languages and knowledge.

During his time at Nebraska and through his leadership, Pound helped shape the University in the study and teaching of law, football, athletics, school spirit, student leadership, and cheerleading. Pound was considered one of the nation's leading legal experts of his time, and he was inducted in the Nebraska Hall of Fame in 1976.

A noted economist, Alvin Johnson, once made a comparison of the two famous siblings: "Louise Pound, modest and extremely talented sister of the great Roscoe—Louise, who doesn't know to this day that at least one person considers her greater still." Even considering his many accomplishments, Roscoe would comment, "Around Nebraska I'm known as Louise Pound's brother."

Louise Pound—Professor, Athlete, and Champion of Equal Rights for Women

Emma Louise Pound (1872–1958) was the legal name stated on her University of Nebraska diploma, but, like her brother, she was known by her middle name. Louise Pound was an accomplished educator, scholar, athlete, author, folklorist, and linguist. She dedicated her life to writing, her studies, her students, athletics for women, causes for the advancement of women, and the University of Nebraska.

Pound supported equal rights for women and women's suffrage concerning the right to vote, but dear to her heart was making sure female students had the same opportunities as men on campus. Pound did not fit the Victorian mold; she was impatient, intense, a fast-paced ball of energy who wasn't afraid to break barriers, play by her own rules, and speak her mind. As a brilliant, confident woman, she would stand up for her students and colleagues, even if doing so had consequences that hurt her in the eyes of the University and hurt her career. Pound's accomplishments did not stop in the classroom; she was also an amazing athlete. Mentally and physically she was a force to be reckoned with in Lincoln and on the University campus.

Louise was born in Lincoln, Nebraska, on June 30, 1872, to a father who encouraged her athleticism and a mother who promoted education and equality. At an early age, Pound was instilled with a belief system that encouraged personal excellence, holding in high regard the achievement of individuals. It was this belief in excellence that influenced everything she touched and how Pound lived her life. She was educated at home until she entered the University of Nebraska preparatory school at the age of fourteen. Pound's upbringing and inner drive led her to be aggressive and competitive, and she took these qualities with her to the University.

In her biography of Louise Pound, author Marie Krohn said, "She played games to win, and she studied to excel. Another motivation for her excellence was her continued desire to keep pace with Roscoe."

As Roscoe Pound was creating organizations and leading the direction of the University male students, Louise Pound was making sure female students also had equal opportunity. An example of the competition between siblings was shown when Roscoe, as a student, was involved in a military cadet drill team. Like Roscoe, Louise helped form a military drill team in 1888 for women. The women wore uniforms and carried the same heavy rifles as the men. She had an intense desire to compete with her brother, not only for herself, but for all women, to demonstrate what was possible.

This rivalry was again shown in the football stadium in 1901 when Roscoe was assisting the males in forming cheering sections and by the fall of 1903 when Roscoe had organized the Innocents Society to take charge of leading cheers on the field and school spirit on campus. By 1904, Louise was making sure female students would have their own separate cheering sections and not have to rely on being escorted by a male to attend a football game. By the fall of 1904, the female students had banded together to organize the first separate female cheering section in the stadium, with the assistance of Louise Pound and Mrs. Clapp, the head of the physical education department.

Pound Organizes First Female Cheerleaders

With World War I raging in Europe during 1917, there was a shortage of men on campus, which prompted Pound to begin to focus her attention on female students cheerleading on the field with men. The timing seemed ideal and a natural transition for the females to cheer on the field, due to the past success of the female cheering sections. In 1917, to prepare the women to lead cheers while joining the men on the field, Pound organized the Valkyries, a junior-senior women's group, to promote opportunities for women in activities on campus. Pound and the Valkyries produced the first female cheerleaders at the University of Nebraska. In fact, this was the first time that any college had ever had women cheering on the field.

Although Louise and Roscoe shared many similar talents, Louise's natural abilities clearly exceeded her brother's in the area of athleticism. Their mother, as a young child, had shown signs of being naturally athletic, and their father had played baseball in college. So Louise Pound's athletic abilities were inherited, and her family members recognized this fact when pointing out that she was the athlete in the family. Ed Weir, a star football player at Nebraska, once stated, "That whole Pound family is outstanding. And Louise—Hell, kid, she may be the finest athlete, male or female, that Nebraska ever produced."

Pound relished athletic competition, and that passion pushed her to excel and win, especially when playing men. Contrary to general impression, there is no reason to believe Pound disliked men. She had many male friends, but she did enjoy beating men in athletic competitions. She made her own path and wasn't afraid to bend or break gender lines. "She excelled at every sport she attempted, and she attempted them all," according to Robert Cochran, a professor of English at the University of Arkansas whose 2009 biography is *Louise Pound: Scholar, Athlete, Feminist Pioneer*.

During the Victorian era, lawn croquet was a popular game. Pound had mastered lawn croquet by the age of fourteen, but considered it too tame of a sport. She was drawn to demanding sports involving an athletic challenge, so she taught herself tennis in the 1880s, just as the first tennis courts were being installed in Lincoln.

In 1890, at the age of eighteen, Louise Pound became Lincoln's first tennis champion, victorious on a dirt court, and beating male opponents. The competitive and physical nature of tennis appealed to her, and tennis became her favorite sport. "From the beginning of the game's introduction to the United States, women participated in the sport. Louise Pound broke no gender barriers in playing tennis, but she did become a local celebrity as the first female member of the Lincoln Tennis Club," according to Krohn.

Pound continued her victories in 1891 and 1892, winning the Nebraska women's state singles championship. While a student at the University, Pound achieved numerous athletic accolades. She dominated University tennis claiming the University of Nebraska men's singles and doubles championships. In 1894, she won the intercollegiate championship in mixed doubles. Pound partnered with Charles Foster Kent of Yale to win the men's doubles championship of Wayne County, NY. She was the only woman on the University men's varsity tennis team and was awarded a men's "N" letter for her intercollegiate play.

Louise Pound as a University of Nebraska faculty member wearing her varsity "N" letter sweater in 1925. As a student she had earned a varsity letter in men's tennis and women's basketball.

Louise Pound was a champion tennis player starting in 1890 and into the turn of the century. She was a champion in many sports, but she considered tennis her favorite.

In 2018, the University of Nebraska athletic department finally recognized Louise Pound as a men's "N" letter winner and has included her as the only woman to be a part of the men's "N" club and very likely, in the future, to be the only woman ever to be so honored with membership into this exclusive male club.

"As a natural athlete, she ignored the physical constraints placed upon women during the Victorian era and competed against men in tennis. Making a name for herself by getting involved in male dominated fields of sports and scholarship, Louise joined the ranks of the 'New Woman' who ignored gender restrictions," wrote Krohn.

"The 'New Woman' emerged in the 1890s and sparked controversy throughout the years and into the 1920s. They came from both the working class and elite society. Shunning the home-centered roles of their mothers, they were sometimes aggressive in their quest for self-fulfillment through education and careers. Often their chosen occupations invaded fields dominated by men," according to Krohn.

The bicycle was a symbol of the "New Woman", giving them a newly acquired freedom in transportation and in their clothing styles. Also, smoking was a behavior associated with this new freedom. Pound was known to smoke a little, but she made sure to point out that she did not inhale. This new era occurred right at the time when Pound was a student at the University of Nebraska and was developing into a young woman.

She immersed herself in the University and developed many strong, like-minded friendships. At a slender 5 feet, 5 inches tall, Pound was a beauty, and she had a striking appearance with her petite stature, brown eyes, reddish-brown, up-swept hair, and an oval face. She attracted the attention of men on campus and also captured the attention of a young Willa Cather. As "New Woman" advocates and University students of similar interests and intellect, Pound and Cather quickly connected as friends. Their literary and writing interests brought them together to share the editorship of a literary journal called *The Lasso*—a literary tool designed to support school spirit.

As a University student, Pound involved herself in extracurricular activities. She enjoyed joining and creating clubs and organizations and typically became the leader. She enjoyed having a good time, socializing, parties, music, the theater, playing bridge, dining out with friends, and dancing. Also, she belonged to the literary society called the Union, which was another one of her passions. Louise Pound and Willa Cather shared this passion and were both actively involved as sergeants of arms for the Union. In 1892, Pound was Union president. She wrote and acted in plays with her friend Cather. Both women were close to their brothers and rejected traditional female roles, which further helped bond them as friends. The women remained close friends from 1891 to 1894.

Even though the friends had similarities, they were different in notable ways: Cather displayed a masculine demeanor and was intrigued by Pound's strong, athletic, intellectual, yet soft side. Cather styled her hair in a short cut and wore boyish clothes. Cather was not a favorite of many of her fellow students because she was outspoken and opinionated. Pound enjoyed the company of a like-minded friend, but she didn't share in Cather's deep attachment and feelings. Cather became increasingly demanding of Pound's time and attention.

Their friendship ended after Louise's brother, Roscoe, returned to Lincoln from Harvard. Roscoe had become acquainted with Cather through her friendship with Louise and her visits to the Pound family home, and they knew each other as students on campus. Both Roscoe and Cather were strong-willed, outspoken personalities, and there was always a tension that existed between them.

It is unknown what sparked Willa Cather to strike out, but in 1894, she wrote a damaging article in *The Hesperian* school newspaper in the March 10 edition, titled "Pastels in Prose." In this article and according to Marie Krohn, Cather made comments about Roscoe, calling him a "notorious bully in his youth, who now bullies mentally just as he used to physically" and saying "he hung around the University only to brag about himself."

The entire Pound family banded together, and Willa Cather was no longer allowed in the Pound home. Louise's loyalty to her family was her top priority, and she ended her association with Cather.

"The end of the friendship probably was inevitable," wrote Krohn. "It would have been impossible to give Willa the affection she demanded." After college, Cather settled out east becoming a famous and successful novelist.

The Rise of Women's Athletics

From 1891 to 1900, under Chancellor James Hulme Canfield's leadership, the University of Nebraska administration followed an innovative path leading into what was considered the Golden Era—a developmental time of high energy, ambition, and high hopes on campus. Canfield, an idealist and forward thinker, was an admired leader who traveled the state as a popular speaker and charmed everyone he met. During his reign as chancellor, the University of Nebraska was one of the top four state universities in the country, along with Michigan, Wisconsin, and California. Chancellor Canfield's daughter, Dorothy Canfield, was a classmate and close friend of Louise Pound. They had similar interests, and, later, Dorothy Canfield Fisher would become an accomplished and successful novelist and writer.

Chancellor Canfield raised a strong daughter who had a lot in common with Pound. The chancellor was in favor of supporting the advancement of women on campus. In 1891, during his first year as chancellor, Canfield created the department of physical education, appointing a young Lincoln woman, Anne Barr, as a class leader of the department. Women's athletics at the University were now boosted and supported by Anne Barr. While a student, Pound assisted her friend Barr and volunteered with the physical education department. The position was a natural fit for Pound due to her interest and ideals in athletic competition. Together they expanded the sports program.

Anne Barr introduced basketball for women in 1896 at the University of Nebraska. When basketball was introduced to collegiate women, it was a controversial sport because it was considered a rough sport for the Victorian period. Barr was the starting center and captain of the women's basketball team from 1897 to 1899. Pound also played on the team until the end of the 1898–1899 season. The women made a shocking debut because they wore bloomers on the court while playing basketball, and at times males were not allowed to watch the games.

When basketball was first introduced at the University, the female students took an immediate interest, more so than the males. No doubt this interest was because of the involvement of Louise Pound. In 1897 she organized, managed, coached, and played on the women's basketball team. The following year, the women's basketball team played their first intercollegiate basketball game against Council Bluffs.

Pound became well known as a basketball player and coach. During her ten years of coaching, the team was successful, popular, and profitable. Pound's basketball teams disregarded the women's rules and, of course, played by the men's rules. The women's basketball games were so popular that, when they played Minnesota, the game drew a crowd of 5,000 fans, including the governor of Minnesota and the University Band.

Krohn reported, "In an interview, Louise commented on the games, saying 'Oh nothing much happens as a rule. Sometimes there's a dislocated wrist or collar-bone, a black eye, a cut on the lip, a broken finger or some little thing like that but I never saw anything serious happen.'" In recognition of her accomplishments in basketball, Louise lettered and was awarded a varsity "N" from the University.

After the success of the women's basketball team, Barr expanded the sports program at the University by making tennis, track and field, and then gymnastics available to women. In 1908, soccer and swimming were established as sports for women, although they remained intramural. The University was among the first schools to open such wide athletic opportunities for women, no doubt because of Pound's influence. And she wasn't done yet.

As women were discovering sports, Louise Pound formed elite teams and encouraged women to play rough intercollegiate athletics. Her female mentality was not typical during the current Victorian times; men's sports emphasized winning, and Pound surely believed you played to win. Starting in 1904, there began to be a reprisal of the concerns of women's health issues and the effects of competitive sports. The University's dean of women, Mrs. Edna M. Barkley, was against basketball because of the potential health effects and eventually ended intercollegiate basketball for female students.

"When outsiders and a few others protested that girls were 'too frail of health' and 'too easily upset emotionally' to engage in competition in athletic sports, Nebraska's intercollegiate and other matches were given up," Louise Pound said. Such notions didn't curb her athleticism as Pound taught herself to figure skate (the first female in Lincoln to do so on frozen ponds); she introduced downhill skiing to Lincoln despite the challenge of finding a hill in the flat city; and she held the Lincoln high-diving record, set records in rifle target shooting, and participated in horsemanship, bowling, and softball.

Louise Pound, pictured with her Rambler bicycle, was a decorated cyclist. She altered her Victorian clothing style to accommodate riding a bicycle.

Pound was one of the first to own a bicycle in Lincoln. She didn't let the constraints of Victorian clothing hold her back; she changed her clothing styles to be more comfortable and manageable to ride a bicycle, resulting in hiking up her skirt to midcalf length. Bicycling brought mobility and freedom to women and helped change their lifestyles. In 1896, according to suffragist Susan B. Anthony, "Bicycling has done more to emancipate women than anything else in the world. I stand and rejoice every time I see a woman ride on a wheel. It gives women a feeling of freedom and self-reliance."

Pound was a member of the Century Club and in 1906 received awards for cycling one hundred continuous miles in a twelve-hour period. According to Krohn, "She also earned a Rambler Gold Medal for riding an unbelievable 5,000 miles in one year, an accomplishment that gave her a membership in the Century Road Club of America." This was an amazing cycling accomplishment, even by today's standards, and it was done all while wearing long, cumbersome skirts, stockings, and lace-up dress shoes, on a one-speed bicycle riding on rough, mostly dirt roads.

Once Louise Pound was physically unable to perform at a level that suited her competitive nature and now with problems caused by wearing bifocal eyeglasses, she gave up tennis and took up the game of golf as soon as it arrived in Lincoln. She quickly excelled at the sport, which replaced tennis as her new favorite. She was a top-ranked golfer in Lincoln between the years of 1901 and 1927.

She finished playing golf and gave up her athletic career around the early 1930s when she was ready to retire from sports and may have felt the game of golf was turning soft. Nellie Yost once reported Pound stating, "Golf seems to be getting sissier [sic]. I see them riding around the course in electric carts now."

Breaking Rules for Women in Sports

Throughout her lifetime, Louise Pound opened the door for women in sports, broke rules, and set new boundaries while achieving wins, medals, and records in a variety of sports. In recognition of her athletic feats, in 1917, Louise was awarded a life membership into the University of Nebraska's Women's Athletic Association. In 1955, Pound was the first woman named to Nebraska's Sports Hall of Fame, achieving this honor at the age of eighty-two. Also, as recently as November 2015, the *Omaha World-Herald* published its list of Nebraska's 100 greatest athletes, and Louise Pound was ranked number eighty-six.

Pound graduated from the University at the top of her class in 1892 with a bachelor of letters degree and a degree in music. The Phi Beta Kappa chapter had recently been established on campus, and Pound was one of the first members. Her Phi Beta Kappa key was engraved in Latin with *sedeant pueri*—which, knowing his sister, amused Roscoe to translate, "Let the boys go back and sit down."

The University was progressive in forming the first graduate program established west of the Mississippi River. Pound entered the University of Nebraska graduate school in Lincoln and in 1895 earned a master's degree in philology (philology is the study of languages and their historical origins and meanings). She received a diploma in piano as well as in music theory and harmony. However, her professional interest was in the English language and literature, leaving music only for personal enjoyment.

Upon graduation with her master's degree, Louise Pound was hired by the dean of the College of Arts and Sciences, Professor Lucius Sherman, and began her teaching career as an instructor in the English department.

During the summer months of 1897 and 1898, she traveled to the University of Chicago to take classes to further her education. While on the road pursuing educational opportunities, Pound continued conquering opponents on tennis courts where she continued to win prestigious tournaments and championships against the best players of the world.

Professor Sherman encouraged Pound to continue her education and assured her of a job in the English department when she completed her PhD. At the turn of the twentieth century, one unwritten consideration for admission to a graduate program was based on gender, making it difficult for women to be accepted and continue their education and careers. Pound found this to be true when seeking admission for her doctoral study. Germany was well known for their outstanding graduate programs, and this is where she focused her attention. Pound first applied to Leipzig University in Germany, but she was declined admission.

"No college would accept her as a doctoral candidate, so she went abroad, studying at the University of Heidelberg, where she earned her doctorate in 1900," according to Walt Sehnert at the McCook Gazette. Her brilliance and determination impressed and perplexed the academic Europeans. If her goal to complete her PhD in two semesters instead of the usual seven wasn't lofty enough, it had to be achieved at the same time she was becoming proficient in the German language.

While in Heidelberg, Pound's focus was not strictly academic, as she continued her athletic pursuits to challenge herself and conquer opponents. For leisure she ice-skated and snowshoed, and she hiked in the mountains around Heidelberg. In Germany, she played on the women's cricket team with American and English students. While she was a member, the team beat the men's cricket team for the first time in school history. One can only imagine the pleasure she derived from this victory. In 1899, she won the tennis championship of Heidelberg and then won again in 1900. Also, while in Heidelberg, she played a tennis match against the incumbent German men's Olympic champion with the match ending in a draw.

Pound's dissertation titled "The Comparison of Adjectives in English in the XV and XVI Century" was written in German. The reason for her goal to earn her doctorate in one year is unknown; maybe she was anxious to return to Lincoln to fill the job promised to her before any changes took place or maybe she was simply setting high standards for herself to achieve the unachievable. Although at times she doubted the goal she set for herself based on prevailing attitudes toward gender, Louise Pound accomplished her goal within one year, returning to Lincoln with her PhD in hand, magna cum laude.

A Clear Career Choice for Miss Pound

As promised, she joined the faculty to teach American literature, contemporary English, and comparative literature. Pound focused on her career at a time when most women were busy attracting husbands and thinking about a family. It was an expectation for women to choose either a career or a family, since it was not an option to do both. Pound's decision to follow a career path was a clear choice for her.

Louise Pound and her sister, Olivia, lived in their childhood home, and after their parents passed away, they inherited the home and continued to live together as roommates the rest of their lives. Olivia was a teacher in Lincoln, joining the faculty of Lincoln High School in 1897. Later she was named assistant principal and held the position until her retirement in 1943. Both women choose careers over marriage.

As a professor, Pound always made herself available to her students. It was Pound's nature to be drawn to and ready to help others. Her female students saw her as a role model—they were loyal to her and adored her. Her students always knew her as Miss Pound—a title she preferred over Dr. Pound. As a professor and athlete, she took special interest in helping her female students succeed in the classroom and on the playing field. She influenced and paved the way for University co-eds to experience equal opportunities in education, athletics, and cheerleading.

In the early twentieth century, Pound's career was thriving. She had firmly established her reputation in academics and was one of the most prominent females in America. As a trailblazer, she had many firsts to her credit, which included being one of the first female professors in America. Also, she was the first University of Nebraska female graduate to receive her PhD.

The University's 1900 fall enrollment had grown to 2,200 students. In December of that year, an opportunity presented itself for Anne Barr, when Dr. Hasting resigned his position as head of the physical education department. Barr was promoted to acting head of physical education for both men and women.

Also in 1900, a change in leadership occurred at the University with Dr. Andrews accepting the chancellorship. The year of 1900 seemed like a magical year: the stars had aligned for women on campus: Anne Barr was promoted to preside over the physical education department; Louise Pound was beginning her career as a professor at the University; and both Barr and Pound had the continued support of a new chancellor. The efforts of Barr and Pound over the next eight years opened the door for opportunities and set an example for women in competitive intercollegiate athletics on the University of Nebraska campus.

The hiring of Chancellor Andrews was a positive influence on campus with his efforts to expand the University. Pound supported Andrews's leadership for his forward thinking and the positive direction he was taking the University. Andrews supported the advancement of football at the University.

"An avid competitor, Louise approved the elevation of the football team and cheered for their victories from the stadium, but football wasn't a sport that women played," Krohn reported. She loved football as a spectator sport and attended University of Nebraska football games, claiming not to have missed a game in over thirty years. In the early years of football, when many questioned the brutality of the sport, Pound embraced it as a game. Football was a sport that women were not allowed to compete in, and this bothered her. She discovered the closest sport to football and helped bring soccer to campus, since it was claimed to be the football of England. She organized the first women's soccer team at the University.

Anne Barr presided over physical education until 1902 when R. G. Clapp, MD, an athlete from Yale, was hired to take over the department. Dr. Clapp married Anne Barr in 1903, and the couple dominated physical education at the University of Nebraska over the coming years. Anne Clapp resigned in 1908 following the birth of their daughter, as a tendered resignation was an expected course of action once she was a mother. The prevailing mind-set considered it impossible for a woman to raise a family and run a household while pursuing a career. Upon her departure, her husband, Dr. Clapp, directed women's physical education, while Louise Pound assisted as an unofficial sports mentor.

The friendship and support Louise received at the University would shift in 1908 when Chancellor Andrews left his position. The position was offered to Roscoe Pound, but he declined, knowing his future belonged to the advancement of law and working closely with students. The head of the chemistry department, Samuel Avery, took over leadership of the University, and under him the women's physical education department began to slowly deteriorate. By 1918, it was to the point where action needed to be taken to revive the department.

Pound struggled with some members of the University's administration. They were under the impression she didn't know her place and found her intimidating. She spoke her mind and wasn't afraid to challenge authority at the University, actions that didn't always sit well with the administration. Krohn stated, "Assuming a combative stance against University administrators—as though they were opponents on a tennis court—gave vent to Louise's competitive spirit." According to historian Knoll, one administrator said that Louise Pound "took ten years off his life." Knoll was also quoted as saying, "The women whom she sponsored were not advanced because deans were afraid they would become as difficult as Louise Pound."

The strides taken by the "New Woman" movement began to stress societal norms; men felt pressure as more women opted for careers, and female professors had a difficult role due to the attitudes of their male counterparts. The newfound freedom of women may have struck fear in society and challenged norms—examples were that female students no longer relied on escorts to football games; women were cheerleaders next to men on the field at football games; women wanted careers outside the home; and women had won the right to vote.

In the setting of the times, World War I had ended, and men were coming back to the University either as students or back to their careers. Prohibition and then the stock market crash brought about budget cuts that found the University of Nebraska with decreased funding as well as changing attitudes. Victorian values were making a comeback. Physicians began discussing the concerns of strenuous athletic activity compromising women's reproductive organs and the overall health of women.

Not only was this consensus felt at the University of Nebraska, it also had spread nationwide. A general segment of the population felt threatened with the increased competition of females for careers and the disruption of home life; they maintained that women should be at home taking care of households and families.

Louise Pound was a strong woman with strong views, but she could not combat this social change and national movement. Pound was in favor of and believed in intercollegiate sports opportunities for elite, gifted female athletes, and she wanted the field of women's athletics to continue to grow from where it had already progressed. She and her contemporaries had successfully fulfilled her vision from 1895 until 1924.

POUND CHALLENGES MABEL LEE

Then Mabel Lee arrived on campus in 1924 and everything changed.

As the tide was changing back toward Victorian thinking, Chancellor Avery hired a new head of the women's physical education department to revamp the program after finding his ideal candidate in Miss Mabel Lee. When interviewing for the position of head of physical education, Lee impressed Chancellor Avery with her ladylike demeanor, her college training, her professional career résumé, and her theories in physical education for females. Lee had an interest in working harmoniously alongside men rather than competing against them. This, in combination with her Victorian values, appealed to the administration at the University of Nebraska. To Avery, she seemed the perfect fit for the University to fill a need for the campus.

And then Lee ran into the buzz saw known as Louise Pound.

When news spread on the University of Nebraska's campus concerning the hiring of a highly trained professional to take over the women's physical education department, Louise Pound was elated. The elation quickly turned sour when Pound discovered Lee's views on sports. Pound and Lee were on extreme opposite ends of the spectrum with Lee supporting mild play for all women and Pound supporting elite competition for the most gifted women. Pound viewed Lee's mild, tame theory of sports as "sissy" athletics. Also, their views contrasted in that Lee did not consider herself a feminist, nor did she support the suffrage movement.

Upon arriving at the University, Lee quickly noticed the effect of football on the rest of the school. She came to view the men's department and football in particular as having special privileges. She developed a lifelong disgust of football, which caused her to separate herself and her program from the men's program.

Even though their differences ruled their tense relationship, Pound and Lee had many commonalities. Both women were very stubborn, believed in physical education, were accomplished, respected professional women in their respective fields, were the first women presidents in major professional organizations, were published authors, devoted themselves to their careers, and never married. They were, instead, devoted to their students and considered them like their families.

Pound was inducted into the Nebraska Sports Hall of Fame in 1955 for her accomplishments as an athlete. Much later, in 1979, Lee was inducted into the Iowa Women's Sports Hall of Fame for her work in physical education. And both had buildings on the University campus named after them.

The personal and professional divide between Louise Pound and Mabel Lee lasted the rest of their lives, and they never settled their differences. Lee had an upper hand on Pound since she was head of the physical education department. Pound held no influence since she was in the English department. Lee also had the full support of the administration, which was the ultimate bottom line.

The hiring of Lee, in combination with Professor Sherman's retirement in 1929, caused Pound to lose support with the administration. The administration listened to her out of respect (and probably fear) but turned a deaf ear to her requests. Pound had powerful family and friends and could not be easily dismissed, but she was now held in her place going forward. Pound had always felt confident challenging the system, due to her upbringing and being surrounded by the strength of her family name; however, by this time her father had long passed away, Roscoe had lived out east for several years, and her prominent support system was vanishing.

"Although they could not dispense with her services or ignore the prestige she brought to the University," Krohn reported, "Louise Pound's superiors employed subtle ways of punishing her for questioning their policies. In fifty years of teaching she was never chosen to head the English department, nor did she receive sabbatical leave, a grant-in-aid, or carfare to professional meetings."

In 1972, the federal government stepped in, and dramatic change happened involving women and intercollegiate athletics. In her master's thesis, Kristi Lowenthal stated, "Title IX of the Education Amendments act of 1972 prohibited discrimination on the basis of sex by universities and other schools receiving federal funds; in essence allowing women to form fully funded varsity teams."

Louise Pound had passed away in 1958 and never witnessed the passage of Title IX legislation. Title IX represented her views and further proved that her opinion of women in elite athletics and competition was correct. Title IX was a final victory for Louise Pound over Mabel Lee and would have delighted Pound, validating her beliefs of intercollegiate athletics for women and further proving she was a woman ahead of her time.

As for Mabel Lee, she retired from the University of Nebraska in 1952, but lived another thirty-three years, passing away in 1985. She lived to see her theory about elite, intercollegiate sports for women crumble. However, her stubbornness prevailed as she stood by her views and continued to criticize intercollegiate sports for women. Intercollegiate sports for women became a permanent fixture at the University of Nebraska by the late 1970s.

Pound loved Nebraska and dedicated her life and career to the state, the University, the pursuit of personal excellence, and most of all to her students. She encouraged her students in their educational and extracurricular activities, as a professor and advisor. Pound had a sharp wit about her that made a lasting impression, and she was beloved and cherished by many of her colleagues, friends, and students.

Louise Pound was held in high esteem nationally and internationally and probably would have reached the high point of her career at another university, but she chose to stay loyal to the Nebraska she loved. Nebraska was where her home, family, and heart were located, and she chose to reside there her entire life. Pound was a professor at the University of Nebraska for fifty years and retired in 1945, and by that time had published more than 200 articles and books. As was her brother Roscoe, Louise proved to be a prolific writer. In considering her many scholarly and athletic accomplishments, she was most proud of her work and guidance with students in the study of language, literature, and folklore.

Cheerleader Ed Dosek in 1940.

An illustration of her academic priority was shown at the end of the school semester in 1940 when the football team had a winning season and was invited to play in the Rose Bowl against Stanford University. The city was celebrating the announcement, and on campus, cheerleader Ed Dosek was running around campus entering classrooms to give a cheer and to generate enthusiasm, notifying students of an upcoming parade and rally.

According to Cochran and recounted by Dosek, several years later, "I broke into her classroom and proceeded to lead a few cheers. It was a fairly large class; I remember it had a sloped floor. Anyway, she didn't take too kindly to that. She shooed me off the stage and reported me to the dean's office…I think she understood my enthusiasm; she was eager to support the team herself. But she was also very adamant about her classroom. That was the point, you see. The schoolwork came first."

In her professional and athletic career, she was honored, received awards, championships, and was accomplished, but in the end what really mattered to Louise Pound was best described by Krohn: "Passing on the flame of learning to her students and the general public through teaching, writing, and speaking, in addition to helping friends, colleagues, and students, reflected the generous spirit of Louise Pound and enriched the lives of those who came in contact with her."

Buildings can be built and torn down, but the legacy of Louise Pound and her brother, Roscoe Pound, remains indelibly written into the history of the city of Lincoln, the University of Nebraska, and the athletic department—as they embodied the true spirit of Nebraska.

Louise Pound in a studio portrait in her later years.

The Secrets of the Innocents Society

The Innocents Society, UNL's first honorary society, is unique to the University of Nebraska. Prior to the Innocents being established, the University was forming its identity and professors were also the student leaders. The professors stepped up to lead because it was difficult to keep the interest, stability, and momentum of an activity to move forward without a student organization in charge. According to Innocents's former Secretary Howard G. Allaway, "Until the Innocents Society was organized, there had been no medium for organizing Cornhusker spirit or for directing it into proper channels. The Society first furnished the agency to do this."

The time had come for change at the new University, and it became necessary for the professors to place the leadership of the society in the hands of a few intelligent, involved, and hard-working students. Dr. Roscoe Pound said, "The very purpose of its existence was to advance university interests at every possible point; to furnish a compact corps of harmonious workers, where college spirit and enthusiasm might be generated; to give a body of men who would be pledged to put their shoulders to the wheel in all university

Mephistopheles's head above crossed tridents, the symbol of the Society of Innocents, a senior honorary society that originated in 1903.

undertakings; to be a guiding central body to lead in those things that fail in the University of Nebraska because, being left to the student body in general, the old maxim applies, 'What is everybody's business is nobody's business.'"

The seed for the idea of a University male honorary society originated from Pound's experiences as a student at Harvard. The Innocents Society was modeled after the honorary societies of Harvard, Yale, Dartmouth, and Princeton. An example was Yale's well-known Skull and Bones society, which was established in 1832. The Innocents Society was proposed by Pound and sponsored by Professor George Condra.

Revealing the Black Masques

While Roscoe was creating the Innocents, it was important to his sister Louise Pound to bring about similar opportunities for female students; so shortly thereafter, in 1905, she assisted in creating the Black Masque honorary society for females (later known as Mortar Board, a nationally established honorary society). The other women involved in forming the Black Masques were founder Ruth Wilson, Margaret Gummison, Ruth Woodsmall, and Alice Towne.

According to the records of the Black Masques, "The name, 'Order of the Black Masque,' is credited to Ruth Woodsmall and Alice Towne, and the spelling of 'Masque' to Margaret Gummison. The ritual was written by Mae Thomas, Edna Holland, and Margaret Gummison." The number, thirteen members for the group, was chosen largely because the men had thirteen members each year in the Innocents Society. The Black Masques was started to parallel the Innocents Society. A former member would later reminisce on the history of the Black Masques and stated the organization was a direct response to the men's Innocents Society.

According to author Robert Manley, "The Innocents and Mortar Boards were expected to provide leadership for the student body in all its diverse activities. Before the formation of these senior honorary societies, efforts to promote University loyalty were scattered and haphazard." The Innocents and Mortar Board members each year worked side-by-side harmoniously for the better good of the University.

The Innocents Society was established at the University of Nebraska on April 24, 1903, and announced in *The Daily Nebraskan* on April 25, 1903. This article suggested a need for this organization when it reported the following.

> *Faculty members who are in sympathy with the idea and are interested in giving their assistance feel that this organization, drawn as it is from all colleges and social classes in the University, will serve as a long needed unifying element, since the present arrangement of courses is not conducive to class spirit and tends to leave the student at graduation almost as ignorant of the powers and purposes of his fellow classmen as when he matriculated.*
>
> *[Roscoe] Pound and Condra drew on medieval customs of knighthood, as well as papal traditions, in forming the ritual and heraldry of the society. They named the society for the 13 popes named Innocent, who have historically stood as champions against evil. The insignia is red in color and is a Mephistopheles in profile, atop crossed tridents. The Mephistopheles head represents the evil the society seeks to overcome.*

The purpose of the society has always been to provide campus leadership. As leaders, an original goal of the Innocents was to promote school spirit, which was accomplished by being intricately involved in the promotion of athletic events and cheerleading. One of their tasks identified at their first meeting was to take over and organize cheerleading. The Innocents selected two cheerleaders from within their society, and implementation of an organized plan started immediately during the football season of 1903.

The Innocents Society, as it was originally conceived, was a male senior honorary society. Their original foundation was changed in 1976 with Title IX, which paved the way for the inclusion of women. According to a February 26, 1976, article in *The Daily Nebraskan*, "'Under Title IX of the Federal Education Act of 1972, all UNL organizations that discriminate against sex (except in athletic programs) must change their constitutions by July 21, 1976,' said Ken Bader, Vice Chancellor for Student Affairs."

Upon this announcement, Innocents President Dick Blunk stated, "Last semester, Innocents Society 'regretfully' changed the word 'men' to the word 'members' in its constitution, allowing UNL junior women to apply and be considered." He also said he did not want to discriminate against women, but said Innocents has had an "extremely good heritage" since 1903. In 1976, the Innocents had received sixty nominations for membership, of which twenty-five were women.

The Innocents Society led the Missouri-Nebraska bell exchange, a tradition that ended in 2010 when Nebraska moved to the Big 10.

Today, the Innocents Society is composed of thirteen men and women. The membership has always been just thirteen select students. Students apply in the spring of their junior year and are selected based on scholarship, character, leadership, and service. The Innocents maintain secrecy of their rituals and their meeting place. Society members distinguish themselves by wearing dark glasses and red-hooded pseudo-monastic robes to promote the group as a whole, above their individual identities. The new members are chosen in the spring, and their selection is performed by a process called tapping.

According to historian Knoll, "Their ritual of initiation was built around the seven deadly sins and seven matching virtues." The process of choosing only seniors, assigning secret names, and tapping the members is very common to eastern secret societies on university campuses. The traditional tapping selection process was originated at Yale University.

The Innocents were responsible for initiating, organizing, and leading many activities on campus. Some of the activities and traditions they led or continue to lead are these:

- The Missouri-Nebraska bell exchange: The bell was exchanged between the Nebraska and Missouri honor societies. The bell displayed an "M" for Missouri and an "N" for Nebraska. The final score of the game was engraved on the bell and held by the winning school until the next season's meeting on the field. This tradition lasted until 2010, the last time Nebraska played Missouri before moving to the Big 10 Conference. Nebraska was victorious in the last game played between the schools and currently holds the Victory Bell. The bell is on display in the lobby of the Nebraska Alumni Association building.

- The freshman convocation and beanie distribution: In the early years of the organization, the Innocents conducted the freshman convocation for new students to learn about student life and University traditions. The Innocents distributed the green beanie caps that were required to be worn by freshmen. The color was changed in 1932 to red. This was one of the oldest traditions on campus.

- Campus Olympics: The Innocents were in charge of the annual Olympics, a competition between the sophomore and freshman classes.

- Homecoming decorating contest: The Innocents created and judged a homecoming decorating contest. Many of the campus traditions have long since dissolved, but the homecoming decorating contest is still practiced.

- Established the Student Council in 1914, now known as ASUN (Association of Students of the University of Nebraska), which is still active.

- Buffalo head exchange from 1951 to 1962: This was a contest with the University of Colorado. Mr. Chip, a mounted buffalo head, was the prize awarded to the victorious school after the football game. This tradition came to an end when the buffalo head came up missing. The buffalo head was never found, and the tradition was dissolved.

- Football rallies and torchlight parades.

- Ivy Day: During this day, ivy was planted on campus, along with the reading of the class poem and announcement of the class gift. The location of the first known ivy planted by members of the senior class is on the south side of old U Hall, in 1901. Later, Ivy Day became known as Senior Day when, starting in 1903, the Innocents Society would perform their traditional tapping of their new members for the following year. In 1905 the Black Masques also made their first tap on Ivy day.

- Fete Day: In the late spring, high school students from throughout the state would come to Lincoln for their annual track meet and debate finals. The students received their first welcome to the University and first glimpse of campus spirit.

The Innocents were involved in these activities and more; however, their involvement on campus may be even further reaching than known, due to the secrecy surrounding their organization.

The activities of the Innocents Society were interrupted twice in their history due to war in the 1940s and again in the 1970s. The Vietnam War and the antiestablishment feelings by students affected many organizations on campus during this time. The 1980s brought about a rejuvenation for the organization, which became more focused in their purpose. Each year the group has a different focus for their involvement and accomplishments in order to leave a legacy with the University. Every class of Innocents makes a significant contribution and impact on the students and the University.

Drs. Roscoe Pound and George Condra had a vision in creating the Innocents Society, which helped transform student involvement at the University of Nebraska in the early years. Many of the traditions the Innocents headed up were so successful that they remain in existence today. Interestingly, when I contacted members of the Innocents Society for the writing of this book, they had no idea the organization was so intimately involved in cheerleading early on. Yet the Innocents and cheerleading continue as two of the oldest, most successful campus organizations that have helped establish traditions, school spirit, and excellence at the University of Nebraska.

6

HOW THE SEA OF RED WAS ALMOST A SEA OF OLD GOLD

FANS AND STUDENTS WEAR SCHOOL COLORS TO DISPLAY THEIR LOYALTY TO their university for both athletic and nonathletic purposes. With the advent of college athletics, colors of a university became important to distinguish schools from one another on the playing field. Using colors to represent universities was a new concept in the latter part of the nineteenth century.

Princeton first used the colors orange and black in 1867. Shortly thereafter, prior to the first football game with Princeton in 1869, Rutgers proposed and adopted the color scarlet, and the players wore the color in a handkerchief during the game to distinguish the team from Princeton. Rutgers made the decision on scarlet because it was a vivid color, and at the time fans could easily obtain scarlet ribbon to show support of the team during the game. Harvard established their colors by a vote on May 6, 1875, and Yale decided on their colors in 1894.

Typically, universities have two school colors, and two sets of uniforms. Most college teams in football will wear and emphasize their primary color for home games and the secondary color for away games. The primary color displayed at the University of Nebraska is scarlet or red and the secondary color is cream or white. But these colors weren't the first choice.

The colors that originally represented Nebraska first appeared in 1882. A student named Clem Chase, the editor of *The Hesperian* campus newspaper, was influential in the selection of the original school color: old gold. Roscoe

Pound was also involved in the selection of the first school color, chosen for its representation of the Nebraska landscape at sunset.

On April 15, 1882, *The Hesperian* made this editorial comment concerning the new school color, and the statement was reprinted in an article in *The Daily Nebraskan* dated March 14, 1903:

> *"Old Gold" seems to have become the accepted color of the State University and will figure hereafter conspicuously at all our entertainments. To have some mark, some color like this that we can recognize gives us spirit; we can "follow our colors," and old gold is certainly a pretty one and in some senses symbolic. Is not Nebraska one of the western states where the sunsets are always in old gold? Do not our broad wheat fields show wave on wave of old gold? Here, then, for our college color, and may we never dishonor it.*

This color was used until 1893, when suddenly a problem came to the attention of the University. A sports rival of Nebraska, the University of Iowa, wore the same old gold color. It was not possible, or practical, for two teams who frequently play each other to wear the same colors. It was determined that Iowa used the color prior to Nebraska; therefore, the University of Nebraska decided to change its school color. The movement for change was led by Chancellor Canfield, since Canfield was known to take an interest in football.

By the end of 1893, an emotionally charged mass meeting was held to select a new color. Many high-spirited speeches were given at the meeting in debating the change of the school colors. A committee was formed, and one of the members, Ralph E. Johnson of Lincoln, suggested the colors of scarlet and cream.

When the new color options were presented, the students and faculty agreed with the scarlet and cream colors. From this point forward, these school colors have been embraced by Nebraskans. The color red is commonly worn in Nebraska on a daily basis, but no more so than on football game day, when Memorial Stadium is painted its familiar Sea of Red by loyal fans. And those yells and songs? You bet there's history behind them.

7

"No Place Like Nebraska" — University Yells and Songs

"There is no place like Nebraska, dear old Nebraska U." The sound and the lyrics stir the emotions of loyal Cornhusker fans as they watch and listen to the University of Nebraska's Cornhusker Marching Band. A school's fight song is as much a part of the University's identity as the mascot or colors.

Before a football down was even played at the University of Nebraska, the oldest collegiate fight song, "For Boston" composed by T. J. Hurley, was already being played in 1885 at Boston College.

School songs and University yells became a way to rally students at meetings, athletic games, pep rallies, University events, and gatherings. Prior to football and early on at the University, to create cohesion and loyalty among the students, class yells and class colors were developed. Also, it was believed a strong school song would be something alumni could take with them after graduation to bind them to the University and future gatherings.

The University held a song contest in 1886, and *The Hesperian* stated, "A college song is the long felt want in the locality. For years we as an institution have yearned after a rousing throat-splitting song that would fuse us into a united body and wear out the ground with our enemies." *The Hesperian* printed some of the following songs for consideration.

"Our University" by F. L. Wheeler

O dear to our hearts in the school we attend here.
With co-eds so beauteous. Professors so grim.
And dandy warm halls where we loaf in the gloaming.
And only four blocks from a place to get beer.

O this is a boss place, a boss place for culture.
For mental mansards and Corinthian columns;
We'll bask in its shadow until we go busted.
And then we will quietly slide to our homes.

There was an objection to this song, since there was a reference to beer.

"A College Song" by W. S. Perrin

Hail to thee, college, hail
O, University!
Destined thy dying wail
Never to be!
So long as time shall last,
We will to thee stick fast,
Nor from thee flee.

At the time this song was reviewed, it was felt the song had winning potential because it had the makings of a true college song. However, there was a problem with it because it seemed to be too short for a proper song.

"A College Song" by G. B. Frankforter

If you want an education
Here's the place to get it;
Finest place in all the nation.
And don't you forget it.
Chorus: Here we have fossils of dogs and cats.
Pliocene Monkeys and Tertiary rats.

> Acids and beakers and all such stuff free.
> And a jolly professor of chemisteree.

This song was thrown out of the contest because it had a bias toward scientific courses, and a song had to be for the whole University to bring about unity.

"A Point of Order" by J. R. Foree

> I like a game of foot ball
> With medics on the green.
> I like to play with paper wads
> Whene'er a Prof. is seen;
> But of all the things that come about
> To make the dead alive.
> It is to hear the Prep girls sing
> A song in number five.

This song did not make the cut, since it was felt it did not have the dignity of a college song.

In 1889 the editor of *The Hesperian* campus newspaper declared, "A yell is needed for the students—a genuine western, lung-developing yell. Some genius in the University ought to be able to furnish such a yell." Again in 1892, *The Nebraskan* editor declared, "If the University has a genius he should be singled out and commanded to secure a new and striking college yell." Contests to generate enthusiasm and encourage students to create University yells and songs became popular, and there were regular editorials and articles looking for the right yells and songs for the University.

The first all-school yell at the University of Nebraska was created in 1889.

> **U! U! U - N - I!**
> **VER! VER! VER! SI - TI!**
> **N - E - BRAS - KI!**
> **O - O - O OH - H - MY!**

This yell was created by Frank Manley and James B. McDonald. McDonald was involved in the band as a baritone player and later became a drum major. Manley had experience developing yells when he was appointed by his fellow classmates to create their junior class yell in 1887. The UNI yell made its premiere on April 12, 1889, at a baseball game against Doane College in Crete, Nebraska. On that cold and gloomy Friday night, *The Hesperian* described the first use of the University yell at a sporting event,

> *The special train was crowded with students whose capacity for noise was unlimited. The brass band, the ball club, the University yell, Frank Manley, and H. C. Peterson were on board. We needed the band; the yell was attached to Manley or rather, Manley was attached to the yell, and we were bound to scoop Doane with either the ball club or Peterson or with both. The train started. The students were jubilant. It is twenty miles from Lincoln to Crete, but the students' melody was heard in Crete long before the students arrived. Every few moments some enthusiastic student would arise in his seat and a regular war whoop would follow. We arrived at Crete. Doane students received us with a brass band. The Unis crowded on the platform and Manley was heard, "Now, then, one, two, three, yell!!!" And 200 students yelled: "U-U-U-N-I, Ver-ver-Ver-si-ty, N-e-bras-ki, Oh-o-o-h my-y-y!!" Crete stood amazed. The earth reeled. The yell was initiated. The University yell was ready to be put into action for the start of the first football season. The yell was so popular, it was shouted out day and night around campus at all hours; some worried its overuse would ruin our dearly loved yell.*

The concern about the overuse of the UNI yell proved not to be necessary, since the cheer was yelled in the stadium for several years and was a fan favorite. As football became a popular sport and with the elevation of football competition among universities, the demand and need for more yells and songs increased.

Roscoe Pound wrote two songs in Latin that were heartily implemented in 1890, after the football team's first game and win. The first: *Frigida dies est cum relinquimur, est cum relinquimur, est cum religuimur; Frigida dies, est cum relinquimur.* The second Latin song: *Cum diptulis dersalibus non affecti, non affecti, non affecti sumus. Ad infinitum.*

In April 1893, another plea went out in *The Nebraskan* campus newspaper wanting a University song.

We were looking over a college song book the other day. Page after page of Harvard songs, Yale songs, Princeton, and Williams songs were there, but none from the western colleges and none from the U. of N. We might just as well have a University song as not. With musicians like Lehmer and Pollard and such poets as Tallmadge and Fisher, to say nothing of the girls, we ought to turn out some genuine art gems. We haven't many of the "blest ties that bind" here among the students, and a song is a splendid thing to start with. College spirit needs cultivating. Let's have a song. We shall be glad to submit in these columns for approval or rejection by the students anything anyone will volunteer to compose for a U. of N. song.

It was December 1893, and the University still did not have a proper college song that represented the University and that the students and fans could relate to, except for Roscoe Pound's Latin song, "I feel like…," which was first sung at the football game in 1890.

In the fall of 1893, an editorial appeared in *The Hesperian*.

Where is our University yell? Where are our leather lungs which, of yore, used to be inflated to their fullest capacity while shouting for our alma mater? Where is our pristine enthusiasm and college spirit? Surely, not all gone! It is not enough to be present at the foot-ball games, and to make one of a crowd rushing pell-mell up and down the field on the wrong side of the ropes. The boys should mass together and encourage our team with a hearty, vociferous shout during the progress of the game. A few half-hearted yelps do no good. Volume counts.…

The fault is not with the yell it is with the yellers.… Get together and shout in unison. Shout hard and long, in season and out of season, but shout. The University should never think of going into a game without organized shouters in the crowd. Shouting helps the team wonderfully if it is loud enough to be recognized above the noise of the crowd. See that in the future it is loud enough. Don't merely tell your neighbor to see to it or it will never be done. Yell!

Songs and yells were prepared for the Missouri game in 1895, and printed in *The Nebraskan* newspaper. Here is one credited to H. C. Laughlin and a few more:

"Game Song"

Let every good UNI man come right along.
Come with the foot ball team;
Blow a big horn if you can't sing a song
Blow for the foot ball team.

Chorus

U. of N., U. of N., make it one more.
U. of N., U. of N., don't let 'em score.
Don't let 'em score; make it one more.
Down 'em at Omaha.
We've scalped Sioux City and Denver's crew.
Bully old foot ball team.
We'll make it one more and down Missouri too.
Down 'em at Omaha.

Chorus

Big Wilson and Whippie and King will be there.
And all the foot ball team.
When a touchdown is made and a goal kicked by Fair.
YELL for the foot ball team.

Chorus

Then fling to the breezes scarlet and cream.
Wear it at Omaha.
When King bucks the line we will stand back and scream.
Go for 'em foot ball team.

"Chant Song"

We wear the scarlet;
We wear the scarlet;
We wear the scarlet and the cream,
OH!
We are the stu – uff;
We are the stu – uff;
We are the stu – uff, the people say,
WHY?

Yells prepared for the Missouri game

OAKY WOW WOW!
SKINNEY WOW WOW!!
SKINNEY WOW WOW!!!
WOW OW OW OW!!!!

BRAC A CAX CAX
GO AX GO AX
BRAC A CAX CAX
GO AX GO AX
HOO – ROO HOO – ROO
PARABALLOO
NEBRASKA!
U RAH RAH, U RAH RAH,
HOO RAH, HOO RAH
NE – BRAS – KA.

Additional support for a school song came after the 1900 Nebraska vs. Minnesota game. A group of Minnesota fans came to Lincoln to attend a football game, bringing with them their university band. The music of the opponent's band made an impression on the Cornhusker fans. During this time, Minnesota was a big rival of the University of Nebraska, and the competition continued to intensify. The rivalry set the Nebraska fans on a mission and they were more determined than ever to establish a school song and create yells.

To create a new Nebraska yell, a Nebraska alum suggested using an established Harvard yell and Harvard song, but substitute the word *Nebraska* in place of the word *Harvard*.

Harvard yell with substitution of *Nebraska*

RAH – RAH!
RAH – RAH!
RAH – RAH!
RAH – RAH!
NEBRASKA!

Harvard song with substitution of *Nebraska*

Ne – e – bra – ska
Ne – bra – ska
Ne – e – bra – ska
Ne – bra – ska
And away goes the football team.
Up and down the football field;
You will find them where there's need.
And they're ready when the ball's in play.
Ne – e – bra – ska
Ne – bra – ska
Ne – e – bra – ska
Ne – bra – ska
To the goal goes the football team.

Borrowing songs and yells from other schools was not deemed appropriate by University of Nebraska standards. The college wanted original songs and yells for their fans at football games. On October 18, 1901, *The Daily Nebraskan* published an article about student behavior at games and the importance of the University possessing their own yells: "The point was also brought up that the habit of some students yelling yells belonging to other institutions was one unworthy of the University. It is not right that Nebraska should trespass on others' rights but should use that which belongs to the University only."

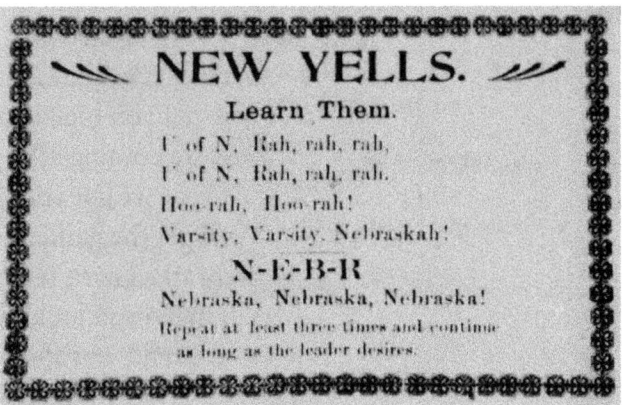

The Daily Nebraskan campus newspaper printed the new yells for the students to learn for games. This notice appeared on October 2, 1901.

During this time, a decision was made to change a portion of the established UNI yell from: Ver – ver – si – ti to Var – var – si – ti. One reason for this wording change was that it just sounded better. Also, it was felt the change in wording would create a more effective yell and would be easier on the fans' throats when yelling.

On October 10, 1901, *The Daily Nebraskan* printed songs and new yells in preparation of the Minnesota game. Here are a few.

Yell #1

U OF N, RAH, RAH, RAH.
U OF N, RAH, RAH, RAH.
HOO – RAH, HOO – RAH!
VARSITY, VARSITY, NEBRASKA!

Yell #2:

Repeat at least three times and continue as long as the leader desires.

N – E – B – R
NEBRASKA, NEBRASKA, NEBRASKA!

Song

Look out you big Norwegians
We're coming after you.
Last year we got your money,
We'll get the game now too.
Nebraska's corn fed players
Will make you look like traps
And send you sprawling,
Loudly bawling.
To your lumber camps.

Chorus
Ne – bra – ska
Fix up the chapel bell.
Ne – bra – ska
Pull the rope like—well.
Ne – bra – ska
Run up the old red light
And let it shine from UNL
Because we'll beat them right.

You'll find your boasted line is
As full of holes as cheese.
And if there are no holes there
We'll make where we please.
You might as well look pleasant,
There's nothing else to do.
And take what Booth's got
Fixed for you—
Another dose of pill.

Chorus
And if a man gets tired
Cap. John don't need to curse.
There're several more just like him,
Or different, which is worse.
We're going to play Northwestern

> Upon thanksgiving; so
> Send off word "Victory"
> O'er the telegraph.
> Back to Ne – e – bra – ska

On October 18, 1901, a vote was taken to have three official University yells to better organize the cheering section:

Yell #1

U – U – N – I
VAR – VAR – VAR – SI – TI
N – E – BRAS – KI
OH – H – H – MY

Yell #2

HOO – RAH – RAH
HOO – RAH – RAH
HOO – RAH, HOO – RAH
NE – BRAS – KA
HOO – RAH – RAH
HOO – RAH – RAH
HOO – RAH, HOO – RAH
NE – BRAS – KA

Yell #3

HIPTA MINNIE GA HOWNIE
GA SOC,
BOOM DA LA NEBRASKA

The third yell was a new yell submitted by an unidentified female student and announced in the October 9, 1901, edition of *The Daily Nebraskan*. The article stated, "This yell was submitted by one of Nebraska's co-ed rooters who says it has been found to work well in small summer vacation parties of Nebraska students. With strong accent on first, third, sixth and last syllables it goes with a first-rate swing and vigor."

Nebraska fans now had a few new yells and songs to follow their team to Minneapolis. Also, the fans showed their support of their team by wearing popular items with the scarlet and cream colors and by sporting accessories such as football buttons, a U of N or Nebraska pennant, a cane with colors, a pennant stick pin of U of N, a streamer of scarlet and cream, and a big megaphone, which they could purchase at the local coop or University Bookstore.

In 1901, U-U-UNI was still popular, and additional cheers were published in *The Daily Nebraskan*. Considering there were many long, complex cheers, students were encouraged to cut out the printed cheers from the newspaper and bring the clipping to the game to aid in their cheering.

Yell #1

GIVE IM THE AX – THE AX – THE AX
GIVE IM THE AX – THE AX – THE AX
GIVE IM THE AX – THE AX – THE AX
WHERE?
RIGHT IN THE NECK – THE NECK – THE NECK
THERE.

Yell #2

MUSH AND MILK AND SUNFLOWER SEED IS THE FOOD ON WHICH WE FEED,
WE'RE NEBRASKA'S AGGREGATION – WE'RE THE HOT STUFF OF CREATION.
OSKEE – WOW – WOW! SKINNY – WOW – WOW! SKINNY – WOW – WOW! WOW!!!

Another opponent of Nebraska's was the University of Kansas. The Jayhawk fans had a popular, menacing yell titled "Rock Chalk Jayhawks." When the yell was introduced, their fans performed it with a resounding impact during games. The yell became an identifying yell for the Jayhawk fans, and "Rock Chalk

Jayhawks" is still performed today. To rival the "Rock Chalk Jayhawks" yell, and in preparation for the next Kansas game, a new Nebraska yell was announced in the November 14, 1901, edition of *The Daily Nebraskan*:

HOO – RAH – RAH
HOO – RAH – RAH
DOWN WITH THE JAYHAWKERS
RAH – RAH – RAH

During the fall of 1906 more yells and songs were added with the already popular U-U-UNI cheer, like the following.

Yell #1

A GROWL
A WHISTLE
HOO – RAY!
NEBRASKA

Yell #2

SAY!
SAY WHAT?
THAT'S WHAT!
WHAT'S WHAT?
THAT'S WHAT THEY ALL SAY!
WHAT'S WHAT THEY ALL SAY?
TOUCHDOWN NEBRASKA!
TOUCHDOWN NEBRASKA!!
TOUCHDOWN NEBRASKA!!

An early, popular song titled "The Scarlet and Cream" was introduced in 1895 and continued to be played by the band for several years.

"Scarlet and Cream"

Sing to the colors that float in the light,
Hurrah for the Scarlet and Cream!
Scarlet the hue of the roses so bright,
And pale is the lily's fair gleam.
Scarlet the east at the breaking dawn,
And scarlet the west when the sun is gone,
Hail! Hail! To the colors that float in the light,
Hurrah for the Scarlet and Cream!

Scarlet the ruby, the jewel so rare,
With colors so brilliant and true.
Pale as the pearl, so bright and so fair,
And clear as the drop of dew.
Bright are our colors, as fair as a dream,
Hurrah for Nebraska, and Scarlet and cream!
Hail! Hail! To the colors that shine the light,
Hurrah for the Scarlet and Cream!

Here's to the college whose colors we wear;
Here's to the hearts that are true,
Hail, Alma Mater, Nebraska so fair!
Hail to our colors too.
Garlands of Scarlet and Cream intertwine,
And hearts that are true and voices combine,
Hail! Hail! To the college whose colors we wear,
Hurrah for the Scarlet and Cream!

A problem arose when *The Daily Nebraskan* discovered and announced "The Scarlet and Cream" song had similarities to Princeton's "Orange and Black" school song. Emphasis was placed on the importance of being original at the University when creating an identity, so because of the similarity, this school song began to lose popularity. Later, as with "Dear Old Nebraska U," similar song issues would arise, but with different results.

Prior to the Kansas Jayhawks game in 1906, *The Daily Nebraskan* encouraged students to cut out and bring to the game this song the newspaper printed in the Friday edition.

Song

Husky Jayhawkers, those wondrous
Talkers
Who always have something to say.
Seem rather nerry in claiming they're
Worthy
To come to Nebraska to play.
They bring with them rooters, bass
Drums and loud tooters.
But when they have vented their
Cheers
The hair of each player from Kansas
Grows grayer
As this from the sidelines he hears:

Chorus

Back to the hay again, Jayhawk
Skidoo – skidoo – skidoo
Your cows are a-bawling your co-eds
Are calling
"Oh, don't let Bill Johnson get thru!"
Schmidt, Cooke, and Chaloupka are
Playing great ball.
And Matters, and Mason you can't stop
at all;
So back to the hay again, Jayhawk.
Skidoo – skidoo – skidoo
(Tune: "Waltz Me Around Again")

In 1909, Robert W. Stevens, an instructor at the Conservatory of Music, composed a song titled "The Cornhusker," and the song's popularity began to increase in 1911. By the 1920s this song had become a favorite.

"The Cornhusker (Come A Runnin' Boys)"

Come a runnin' boys
Don't you hear that noise like the thunder in the sky

How it rolls along in a good old song
From the sons of Nebraski.
Now it's coming near with a rising cheer
That will sweep all foes away,
So with all our vim
We are bound to win and we're going to win today.

Chorus

For Nebraska and the scarlet
For Nebraska and the cream,
Tho' they go thru many a battle,
Our colors still are seen.
So in contest and in vict'ry
We will wave them for the team
And 'twill always stir a Cornhusker,
The old scarlet and the cream.

Robert Stevens had always been a loyal football fan, so in 1942 he gave the copyright of the song to the University of Nebraska.

At the same time two more yells were added to the already popular yells. One cheer was written in 1910 called the "Chant" by Robert D. Scott, a professor at the University. Both Stevens's and Scott's chants worked well together and were often combined. The two chants were commonly performed in unison by the University's men's choir.

Yell #1

**CHEER FOR NEBRASKA,
NEBRASKA MUST WIN.
FIGHT TO THE FINISH,
NEVER GIVE IN,
YOU DO YOUR BEST, BOYS,
WE'LL DO THE REST BOYS,
FIGHT FOR THE VICTORY,
RAH, RAH, RAH.
(REPEAT)**

Yell #2

```
U - N - RAH - RAH
U - N - RAH - RAH
U - RAH - N - RAH
U - N - RAH - RAH
```

Two more yells were added to the two favorites in 1916.

```
OH! YOU! CORN - HUSK - MAN!
RAH! RAH! RAH! NE - BRAS - KAN!
(REPEAT TWICE)
RAY! RAY! NEBRASKA!
```

```
GROWL AND WHISTLE
GROWL
WHISTLE
HURRAY!
NEBRASKA!
```

A change was made when the rooters replaced the typical "Fifteen Rahs" with three "Yea Bo's" with the "Yea" long drawn out and the "Bo" cut short.

On November 30, 1916, *The Daily Nebraskan* reported on the importance of yells and cheering.

Cheering a Potent Force

The value of cheering to a football team is as potent as the value of school spirit, and being concrete, is often productive of more apparent results. The classic story of the famous Yale victory over Harvard when with defeat almost enveloping them, the Bulldogs rallied at the rolling roar of "Brek-ek-kex. Coax" and trounced the ancient foe, has many companion stories in both eastern and western football.

There are those who attribute the victory of the weaker Kansas team over the Cornhuskers two weeks ago to the organized expression of the fighting spirit of the Jayhawk school. For seven years this same spirit has expressed itself in the haunting "Rock, Chalk. Jayhawk": for seven years spirit and cheering along could not cope with invincible prowess. And then came a year when the difference was temporarily not so great that the effect of organized spirit could not be felt: and it was that a weaker team with a stronger spirit won.

The lesson that loyal Nebraskans have learned from the first defeat in four years has been a wholesome one, and it has served to waken the student body and the team to a greater appreciation of the significance of victory. It means, in the opinion of cheerleaders of the past and present, the organization of concentrated cheering at Nebraska into a valuable and powerful factor in deciding victory or defeat. From now on Nebraskans will not be content to rest upon past achievements. With the team they will work shoulder to shoulder for deserved triumph.

It would take several years trying out school songs to discover the ones that would resonate with the students and fans and determine those that were to become the cohesive force needed to unify and to identify with the University. Yells and songs came and went through the years, but when a push was made to publish a Nebraska song book, progress was made for the lasting, time-tested school fight songs.

In the 1920s, the Alumni Association published four Nebraska songbooks. During this time there was a renewed interest in song writing. The reason for the book was to encourage students and alumni to write original songs. As an incentive, prizes were offered of $25.00, $15.00, and $10.00 for the best three songs. In addition to the prizes, every writer submitting a song received a leather-bound copy of the songbook with the writer's name embossed on the cover. A songbook published in 1921 was available at a cost of $1.75.

Nebraska Songs, third edition 1924, stated the following.

> Dear old Nebraska, loyal and true,
> Let us pledge once again our allegiance to you;
> Let us sing of your spirit that never will die,
> But will carry you on with our old battle cry;
> U – Rah – N – Rah – U – N – I
> U – varsity, N – varsity
> Ne – bras – ki. Ne – bras – ki.

To help carry forward the enthusiasm, the spirit, the loyalty reflected by these words, is the purpose of this book. To help preserve in songs worthy of the fine traditions and rich sentiments of Nebraska built through the period of over a half century this book is published.

May its songs help to celebrate many an inspiring victory. May they serve to promote an ever increasing college spirit, a spirit of unity, fraternity, and loyalty. May they continue to make radiant with joy and good fellowship meetings of students on the campus and in the home; of loyal alumni and friends wherever they may get together throughout the world. May its pages grow in number.

In 1930, a new song was written by W. Joyce Ayres titled "Fight Husker Varsity." Ayres became famous six years later, penning the lyrics to the official school song "Hail Varsity." The prelude song, "Fight Husker Varsity," made its debut when printed in *The Daily Nebraskan* on October 31, 1930, and was performed by the Corn Cobs at a Friday evening pep rally.

Nebraska Songs, *one of four songbooks published by Harold F. Holtz, Secretary of the University of Nebraska Alumni Association, in 1922 and Woodruff Printing Company in 1924.*

The next day, at the football game, the band played and the Corn Cobs again performed the song. The song by Ayres resulted when the Innocents Society sent out a request for new songs. Ayres had been an Innocents member when he was in school, and he wrote this song just after graduation. Ayres also wrote the song "Nebraska's Sweetheart."

[Editor's note: Because of copyright restrictions on song lyrics that have not entered the public domain, we are unable to reprint lyrics in full that were written after 1923.]

Interest in song writing continued to be strong in the 1940s and 1950s. The additional interest created increased pressure on the University to establish school songs. Two new songs were introduced by the band at the first football game of 1942. The first song was "March of the Cornhuskers," written by William T. Quick, director of the bands from 1917 to 1936, and M. H. Ribble; the second was "Huskerland," which was written by Harry Minor, a 1908 University alum, and Nat Vincent, a professional songwriter. Both men collaborated with Mr. Helmy on the music arrangement.

A decision was made in 1955 by Vice Chancellor Bruce Nicoll to give the responsibility of the final school song selections to the director of bands, which was a reasonable decision. Out of all the songs written and submitted, three were particularly popular with fans, and selected for the *Nebraska Song* book. The first song selected was "March of the Cornhuskers."

The second song was the now-familiar "Hail Varsity" composed by Wilber Chenowith in 1936 and lyrics by W. Joyce Ayres. Ayres recalled that he

"Hail Varsity" school song.

was paid $5.00 for his work on the lyrics. After the selection of "Hail Varsity," not much was mentioned of "Hail Varsity" until the Orange Bowl game on January 1, 1955. The song had resurfaced and was played during this game. The exposure of the song led to it being adopted as the official fight song for the University of Nebraska and remains so today. "Hail Varsity" is the first song the band plays after a touchdown, with "Dear Old Nebraska U" played next.

"Dear Old Nebraska U" is also known as "There Is No Place Like Nebraska" and "No Place." This song was written by Harry Pecha in 1923.

Gary Steffens, a band alum, had the following to say about the origin of the song.

> *The exact circumstances of its composition are not known, but it is generally accepted that Pecha wrote the song while at Ft. Snelling, Minnesota, for two weeks of ROTC Camp during the summer of 1923. These camps usually gathered students from several schools and, according to students of the time, there was always a night where the various student groups, representing their respective school, would put on a skit. According to legend, Pecha and several of his fraternity brothers presented the song as their skit. While not having been able to completely authenticate the story, I have heard the tale from enough different sources to believe it true.*
>
> *Pecha's own fraternity began using the song during the fall of 1923 and before the football season had ended, it had become popular enough to be listed in the game program with all the other school songs. Billy Quick was fascinated by it and quickly arranged a piano score and band arrangement of it. While the band arrangement was in the original 3/4 time, it was quickly revised to a 2/4 tempo to accommodate marching. It was also included in the fourth edition (1924) of the* Nebraska Songs *book.*

This story, recounted by Gary Steffens, was confirmed when James Marshall was interviewed by *Journal Star* reporter Dick Piersol in an article titled, "Holy Toledo Big Red! Did NU Cop Fight Song?" In the interview Marshall confirmed he was with Harry Pecha, in Fort Snelling, Minnesota, in 1923, as cadets at an ROTC camp. According to Marshall, Pecha changed the lyrics of a song titled "C-H-I-C-A-G-O," which were copyrighted in 1909, to fit a song about Nebraska for the cadet skit. There is another song titled "We're Proud for Toledo," copyrighted in 1906, and all three songs have some similar lyrics. Pecha copyrighted his song in the 1930s. Later the University Male Quartet, which Marshall was a member of, sang the song at a football game. The rest is history for the beloved Nebraska song.

After Pecha graduated, he made an offer to the University of Nebraska to give the copyright of the song to the school in exchange for two lifetime tickets to the football games. Unfortunately, the University turned down his offer, and Pecha gave the rights to the Melrose Music Company of Chicago. Gary Steffens explains as follows.

> *The decision came from the Board of the Intercollegiate Athletics. Board member John K. Selleck remembers. That was an unfortunate decision, but the song had not yet become as popular as it is today and I thought we might set a bad precedent by giving away two lifetime tickets in return for a song. I think we would have been deluged by similar offers.*

> *"No Place" has no official designation among Nebraska school songs. It is simply a song—but a song that…was probably best described by Chancellor Edgar Allan Burnett in a letter to Harry Pecha in 1935. "You probably had little idea of the place you would make for yourself in the hearts of all loyal Nebraskans when you wrote the words and music for 'Dear Old Nebraska U.' Few songs have so endeared themselves, not only to the University family but to the people of the state, as has your song. I have heard it sung on the football field and in gatherings of Nebraskans everywhere. It belongs to the entire state."*

> *One need only see the reaction of the crowd on a Saturday afternoon, as the thundering A flat strains of "Dear Old Nebraska U" echo forth, to know just how true that statement really is!*

History was reversed on October 4, 2008, when the rights to "There Is No Place Like Nebraska" were officially granted to the University during halftime at a Nebraska vs. Missouri homecoming game. The rights were given by alumnus Ted

Sheet music for "Dear Old Nebraska U" or "There Is No Place Like Nebraska".

Randolph, the son-in-law of the late Harry Pecha. In an article by the Nebraska Alumni Association, the story corroborates the origination of the song. Also, according to the Nebraska Alumni Association:

> *Pecha didn't copyright the song until December 18, 1931, giving licensing rights to Melrose Publishing Co. of Chicago. Melrose was bought out by Edwin H. Morris Co., which later was acquired by MPI, Communications. The song is still licensed with MPI, Communications (formerly known*

as McCartney Productions Ltd.), but the University now owns the copyright registration and it will be valid and in force until December 18, 2026 (95 years from the original copyright date). At that time, it passes into the public domain unless the U.S. Congress has taken action to extend copyright agreements.

Randolph requested that the royalties from the song go to the Nebraska Alumni Association.

The song has not been without controversy. School fight songs may be completely original, but it is not uncommon for fight songs to borrow from others. Several universities, along with the University of Nebraska, have similar tunes and lyrics, including the University of Florida, University of Chicago, and the Toledo, Ohio, Public School System.

Another issue is keeping a song's wording current with the changing times and how the meaning of a word may evolve into another meaning. In over ninety-one years since the song was written, the lyrics are showing their age. In 1923, the lyrics "girls are the *fairest*" and "boys are the *squarest*" were commonly used and considered complimentary, but the meanings and use have changed. However, sometimes the charm of tradition keeps the lyrics current. The use of these two words pales in comparison to the meaningful, strong lyrics of "There is no place like Nebraska, Where they're all true blue," and "We'll all stick together in all kinds of weather." These lyrics are the soul of the song and hold the hearts of the fans.

Even though the official fight song of Nebraska is "Hail Varsity," the song "Dear Old Nebraska U" resonates with Nebraskans. "There is no place like Nebraska" is painted in school colors at the entrance of the student Union as a reminder to students.

At a football rally in the fall of 1921, cheerleaders Fred Richards, Dick Kimball, and Ed Shoemaker announced a new way to start cheers, a process commonly used in eastern colleges. The new process began with announcing the cheer, then the cheerleaders shout, "Are you ready, Hip! Hip! Hurray!" followed by the rooters joining in with the cheer.

The chant "Go Big Red" started in the Nebraska stadium in the early 1950s, according to former UNL Sports Information Director Don Bryant, in a personal interview for this book.

Well, historically Cornell University of the Ivy League had been known by its nickname "Big Red," based on Cornell's colors: "Carnelian red, white." However, during the 1950s when Bud Wilkinson's Sooners were running roughshod over all comers, the Sooner fans started yelling "Go Big Red!" and the Oklahoma media picked up on the slogan and began referring to the Sooner team as "Big Red." Nebraska writers—and other conference media—were quick to point out (in our misery over OU dominance) that Cornell was Big Red, not OU! Later, when Nebraska began to compete with the Sooners, our fans started yelling the cry to ridicule the Sooners and it eventually became a yell Nebraskans felt was their real legacy, not Oklahoma's or Cornell's.

Sheet music for "Scarlet and Cream".

There is no denying the yell of "Go Big Red" has stuck with the Cornhusker faithful and is dear to the hearts of Nebraska fans. After every Cornhusker touchdown, the band plays a school song followed by chants of "Go Big Red" echoing around the stadium. Also, pockets of fans randomly around the stadium will start the "Go Big Red" chant during moments in the game to inspire the team.

The cheerleaders' yells from the beginning and into the 1960s had consisted of long, detailed chants. The complicated yells were difficult to learn and coordinate, and the simple yells won over the fans, as was the case with "Go Big Red." The 1960s through the 2000s brought about scaled back yells such as Defense or (Offense) (Repeat); Block that Kick (Repeat); Push 'em Back Push 'em Back, Way Back (Repeat); and of course Husker, Power (Repeat).

The chant "Husker Power" has grown in popularity since its inception in the 1970s. Currently, to start the cheer, a Yell Squad member flashes a sign bearing "Husker" to half the stadium, followed by another sign "Power" held up to the other half of the stadium to create a competitive chant by the fans. The Husker Power chant was taken to this new level in 1982 with Dan Kendig, the former University of Nebraska women's gymnastics head coach. Kendig had been the head gymnastic coach since 1994; however, earlier in his career at Nebraska he was an assistant gymnastics coach from 1981 to 1983. During his time as an assistant coach, he simultaneously coached the Nebraska Spirit Squad. The idea for Husker Power came from his time as a student at the University of Kentucky where the cheerleaders performed a cheer of "Blue White." Kendig thought the cheer would work well at Nebraska so he substituted Husker Power, and the rest is history.

As the crowds grew, a platform with a microphone or blow horn was added and used by the male cheerleaders to assist fan participation with yells.

1948 Yell King, Bill Mickle, motivates the team and fans using a blow horn at a football game.

The male cheerleaders would also use large megaphones to project the yells to the fans. The female cheerleaders' pompons were instruments to orchestrate the timing of the yells. Once males were no longer on the Yell Squad starting in the fall season of 2008, the blow horns and megaphones were no longer used, and it was impossible to direct the fans in cheering.

School fight songs have their place in history and today the rhythm of "Hail Varsity" or "Dear Old Nebraska U" beats through the stadium as the cheerleaders perform with precision routines to the school songs. As with the yells of days gone by, today cheerleaders lead the fans with the current yells of "Go Big Red" and "Husker Power" to inspire the football team. The yells, music, and lyrics pay tribute to the University and endear the hearts and heighten the loyalty of students, alumni, athletes, cheerleaders, and fans.

Through the years, university school fight songs and yells have always been and will continue to be an important tradition for the identification and

Scan this QR Code to hear the song.

Most smart phones have a QR code built into the camera. Simply turn on your camera app and hover over the QR code. You can also hear the recording at www.SpiritOfNebraska.com.

cohesion of school spirit. Among the driving forces behind the school spirit have been the many pep clubs and organizations over the years. Who knew the now infamous Boneyard had its origins in early student sections for men and women and the skull-and-crossbones was created quite by accident? Or that the Blackshirts evolved because of an overstock of black jerseys at a local store during the Devaney era? Those fascinating traditions from Nebraska history are explained in the next chapter.

Photo Album

2016 Yell Squad performing "Dear Old Nebraska U."

UCLA game September 14, 2013, Yell Squad firing up the fans.

Lil' Red and Yell Squad performing at a 2015 basketball game during a time out.

2006 Yell Squad stunting. (Partners from left) Zach Hergert and Anne Marie Rye, Eliot Schwer and Katie Rockwell, Rick Carstens and Kristen Chambers, Andy Richter and Danielle Buehner, John Clabaugh and Shari Kopf, Shaun McAnulty and Shannon Meloy, Eric Widhelm and Adrienne Poppe.

2016 Yell Squad using signs to fire up the fans.

Yell Squad member Geri Finney in 1985 with Herbie Husker.

Yell Squad members Crystal Zabka with stunting partner Mike Siebenthal. Spring game, 2005.

The band performs at the UCLA game on September 14, 2013.

In 1996–1997 the Yell Squad placed second at NCA Nationals in Daytona Beach, Florida.

1996 Yell Squad on the field.

The Scarlets dance team, 2008–2009.

UCLA football game, September 14, 2013. Yell Squad's Jennifer Powell cheering on the Huskers.

1997 Yell Squad performing a sky-high basket toss.

University of Nebraska Band forming the shape of Nebraska.

F

2018-2019 Spirit Squad

1996 Yell Squad stunting on the field at Memorial Stadium.

First home football game of the 2005 season, All Girl Squad: Far left, Catie Menke, Center (Left Base) Ashley Jo Keihner, (Back Spot) Heather Lambert, (Right Base) Emily Heferbrier, (Flyer) Sara Shirk, Far right (Left Base) Amy Jo Blake, (Back Spot) Stephanie Heavey, (Flyer) Lindsey Korth.

Selected Football Program Covers — 1960-2015

UCLA game, September 14, 2013. Yell Squad runs the flags.

At homecoming, 2015, Lisa Belden of LB Photography and mother of Yell Squad member Courtney Belden re-created the 1964 image of Yell Squad females; (Top row, from left) Jean Barber, Diana Focht, Linda Keating, Sandy Stefanisin, Georgia Merriam, Carolyn Daubert, and Becky Haas; (Bottom row, from left) Rachel Samuelson, Kelly Sieps, Brighton Kathol, Bradyn Brownell, Courtney Belden, Megan Gould, Katie Harrison, and Kiara Moody. The 2015 Yell Squad members are wearing their reproduction of the vintage sweaters, which they wear for special occasions.

The 1996–1997 Scarlets dance team at the NCA Collegiate National Championships.

The student section known as the Boneyard at the UCLA game September 14, 2013.

UCLA game September 14, 2013, pregame waving of the "N" flag.

2013 Yell Squad ready for pregame. Jennifer Powell, Alexis Vercher, and Cassie Wilka.

Fan card section at a game on November 17, 2012, flashed messages in honor of former coach Tom Osborne.

The Scarlets ready for game day, September 1, 2012.

The Scarlets dance team at a 2014 basketball game.

The Scarlets dance team, 2013–2014.

Football Press Guide 1964, featuring Pom Squad member Carolyn Daubert.

Football pregame October 27, 2012. Yell Squad ready to perform.

"Cheers for 100 Years," University of Nebraska Spirit Squad Reunion, September 5, 2003.

2006 Yell Squad: (Back row, from left) Eliot Schwer, John Clabaugh, Eric Widhelm, Zach Hergert, Rick Carstens, Andy Richter, Shaun McAnulty, and Chris Peterson; (Front row, from left) Katie Rockwell, Anne Marie Rye, Shari Kopf, Danielle Buehner, Adrianne Poppe, Kristen Chambers, and Emily Dawley.

UCLA game September 14, 2013, Yell Squad performing.

8

OF CORN COBS AND TASSELS — STUDENT PEP ORGANIZATIONS DRIVE SCHOOL SPIRIT

The United States was still in the grips of the Civil War, but in the north, not all eyes were on the war. The first pep club was formed between 1865 and 1870, at the place where American college football originated, Princeton University. The Princeton pep club created the first known cheer.

RAH RAH RAH
TIGER TIGER TIGER
SIS SIS SIS
BOOM BOOM BOOM
AAAAAHHHHH!
PRINCETON! PRINCETON! PRINCETON!

Before pep clubs were organized at the University, however, the Omaha YMCA had challenged the University of Nebraska in football. That was in 1890. In response, *The Hesperian* newspaper reported, "A good opportunity here presents itself to us for making a favorable impression upon the people of Omaha. It would be eminently proper for us to accept the challenge, send the foot-ball team, brass band and yell up to Omaha and surprise the natives of Nebraska's metropolis next Thanksgiving day."

Nebraska's first enthusiastic football fan was Roscoe Pound. He wrote songs in Latin, and then led cheers in the grandstands at that first football game. During the game it was reported, "Great was the applause in the grand stand; and the way in which our yell was rendered astonished the natives, who looked up in amazement to see where such an unearthly noise could come from."

At the turn of the twentieth century, honorary societies, special interest organizations, fraternities, and sororities were popular on the University of Nebraska campus for both male and female students. The University of Nebraska students proved adept in creating large numbers of clubs and organizations, including pep organizations to further enhance school spirit on campus, starting with the development of cheering sections in the stadium.

Pound was instrumental in helping to organize the male students to form rooting squads in the grandstands. The male student pep organization at the University of Nebraska began in 1901 when the male student body became organized at football games to provide more effective yelling. In the fall of 1901, a meeting took place at the Alpha Chi fraternity house to organize male students in sections in the grandstands. In attendance were approximately fifty to sixty representatives from fraternities, literary societies, and any male student interested in attending.

The meeting was led by professors Clements, (Roscoe) Pound, and Wyer. The purpose of the meeting was to organize a rooters club, and Clements was in charge. He felt it was crucial to become organized and to provide support for the football team. Pound agreed with Clements that organization was the key to rooting success.

At the meeting, Pound elaborated on the difference between spirit at eastern and western colleges, reflecting on his experience when he attended Harvard. He emphasized that the lack of spirit was directly related to not having the existence of organized rooting.

"To win, boys," he said, "we will have to get into the spirit of things to make them a success." A plan for the next game was made. All the men in attendance would be divided into four separate squads, and leaders would be appointed for the squads. Each of the men in the four squads was responsible to increase their numbers to fifty by Saturday's game against Ames (later to become Iowa State University) on October 26, 1901, to debut organized cheering.

At the meeting, Professor Clements was appointed as president of the club, and Pound was named head rooter. To encourage the squads in their efforts of best rooting and support for the team, Pound offered a large megaphone as a prize. Also, two hundred megaphones were ordered to aid the rooting sections.

The Daily Nebraskan announcement for students to bring a megaphone for admission to the rooters' section at a football game, 1902.

To further create and support spirit, a rooters' chorus was organized. The choir was directed by Clements and was composed of twenty-four men. The purpose of the choir was to lead and sing the school songs. It was agreed by everyone in attendance that the rooters' club would be made permanent and continue as a tradition.

On October 28, 1901, *The Daily Nebraskan* reported after the game against Ames: "One feature on Nebraska's field Saturday was the rooting. It was a thing not seen by the University for many days—years, it might be added. Four squads under the generalship of Roscoe Pound and captained by Sherman, Shilder, King, and Teach made a noise that would have done credit to the Board of Trade. Squads one and two were on the west benches, three and four on the east side. The squads yelled in rotation thus keeping up a continual fire of howls the game through. The Ames men after the game said the rooting was a revelation to them."

Over the next couple of years, the rooters' club struggled with consistency and leadership. On December 2, 1901, *The Daily Nebraskan* reported, "The lack of enthusiasm at the football rally last Wednesday was decidedly noticeable. The fact that there was no regular chairman was the cause of most of it. The squad leaders were not all in their places and the band had little backing when it struck up songs. The *Daily* would suggest that hereafter a regular chairman be selected beforehand by those who call the rallies."

This sentiment was further supported by the football coach. During a speech by Coach Booth at a mass meeting, he stated, "The team had more spirit than ever before, and that the men would win games when they knew that the University was behind them. What is needed is more organized rooting."

In order to fill the male student rooting sections in 1902, admission to a football game only required male students to bring a megaphone and cheer. It must have been quite a sight to witness hundreds of students in full sections of the stadium, all yelling through megaphones.

Let's Hear from the Women

The cheering sections remained all male exclusively until the fall of 1904. It was at this time the females decided they wanted to become involved too and held their first meeting to encourage female students to attend football games. The first meeting was a success with 500 enthusiastic women in attendance. The women proved to have the proper spirit and enthusiasm to cheer and fill a section of the stadium.

Heading up the organization of the girls' section was Anne Barr Clapp, head of physical education, and Louise Pound. In 1907, the female football section had a supporter in the athletics manager, Earl "Fido" Eager, who made sure the females had a separate, roped-off section in the stadium and encouraged them to bring a megaphone. In 1911, when an enlarged grandstand was completed, Eager again made sure the females had a special section.

Eager's goals in encouraging and supporting the female students to attend football games were to increase gate receipts and create competition between the male and female sections and generate more spirit in the grandstands. As an incentive to increase attendance, the female students were charged a reduced fee for entrance to football games. However, this incentive wasn't really needed as the females enjoyed cheering at games and showed up in large numbers to support the team.

The football coach became involved to assist in educating females on how football was played. He organized a practice game for the women to watch, learn the rules, and practice timely yells. Coach Reed also urged the women to go to the game without the accompaniment of a date. The coach felt that, without a date, women would be less demure and more effective at yelling during the game. This was a shocking idea, since prior to this time females had to be accompanied by a male at football games because it was considered a rough sport.

The unaccompanied females occupied their own section in the north stands, and the male students were stationed in the south stands. The separation in the stands from the males helped to "protect the female students from the rough language," but something unexpected happened with the segregation of the females: the males took this opportunity to express their opinions of the referees and the opposing players.

This behavior was unacceptable and ultimately resulted in the education of the male rooting sections on proper fan behavior. The unacceptable behavior during this time helped in developing the Cornhusker fan etiquette and setting them on the path that would one day lead to their being known as the best fans in college football.

The separated location in the stadium did not deter the females. The separation actually encouraged competition between the sections, and the female students rose to the occasion. The females elected cheerleaders to lead yells and songs at their pregame football luncheons and to lead their cheering sections at games. Before each home football game, the females would gather at a luncheon to rally support for the team with rousing speeches in preparation for the game. Following the girls' lunch, they would hold hands, marching and "snake dancing" in a long line to the field to fill their cheering section.

The informal pep organizations were the beginning of what would later be known as the Corn Cobs and Tassels Pep Clubs at the University of Nebraska. The Corn Cobs, for men, and the Tassels, for women, were created to direct the pep sections in the stadium, and they proved to be successful in organizing pep, developing enthusiasm, and supporting the cheerleaders.

BALLOONS RISE TO THE OCCASION

In 1910, in an effort to organize the leadership of the female cheering section, the Black Masques (later known as Mortar Board), the women's senior honorary society, took charge of the female rooting sections at football games. The Black Masques addressed the matter of the cheering section at each of their meetings to brainstorm ways to contribute spirit and enthusiasm to every game day.

The balloon release tradition had its beginnings in a decision made on October 15, 1910, by

In 1968, the Tassels pep club prepares balloons pregame.

the Black Masques, to add spirit and celebration in the female student section of the stadium. Originally, only the female students released balloons after every score, and today the tradition continues as fans release red balloons in celebration at the first score.

To further their game day spirit, the female student section would be decorated and defined by red bunting and a homemade banner displayed the name of Nebraska. The females carried canes with homemade pennants attached and would wave them during good plays, or they would wave homemade red and white flags. Also, they made and wore capes, using the capes to form an "N" in their section. Other stunts would involve the girls holding red pennants and forming a large scarlet "N" and at different times during the game switch the pennants to white. The female students would strive to outdo the male student section with their colorful spirit.

On October 26, 1914, *The Daily Nebraskan* reported: "Girls show best spirit in years…Never before have the girls been so interested in football as this year, and never before have they given themselves so heartily to the support of the team. This was unmistakably proven by the enthusiastic cheering in the Girl's Section at the game Saturday. They had so much pep as the boys and certainly stood by the team nobly. Who says girls aren't any good at a football game? Anyone who heard the girls cheer and yell at the 'big game' would decide then that the team needs the girls' support and here in Nebraska they get it."

Cheering Sections Merge

In the fall of 1916, the female cheering section was moved from isolation in the north stands to sit in the south stands next to the men's section, but the women were not allowed to commingle with the men. The move of the female student section was made just in time for the Kansas game. The reason for the move of the female students was to include the females as part of the Nebraska spirit and to help increase the rooting for the game.

A strategy was needed for the upcoming football game because the University of Kansas had a reputation for out-yelling their opponents. The competition between the Nebraska side-by-side female and male sections provided more effective cheering. The women had proven themselves in past years as being competent in their cheering sections, and now the combined efforts of the men's and women's sections made a greater impact during the game. Bringing all student sections within close proximity later made sense for both female and male cheerleaders to cheer together on the field.

The years of 1916 and 1917 were particularly instrumental in bringing about the development of organizations for the advancement of women and equal opportunities on campus. Whenever there was a cause for the advancement of women on campus, Louise Pound was at the forefront and actively involved in all matters concerning women students. Pound would take the lead, making sure females on campus had the same opportunities as the men.

In 1916, female students were organizing a Suffrage Club on Lincoln's campus. The students were supported by Mary Graham, dean of women, and Louise Pound, who were both involved in the cause of women's suffrage—supporting the right for women to vote.

The Women's Self-Governing Association (WSGA) was formed to support the advancement of women on campus. The Valkyries (a junior-senior women's group) was established in the fall of 1917 to promote opportunities and activities for women on campus. The Women's Athletics Association (WAA) was formed in 1917 by the Valkyries, and it supported athletic opportunities for females at the University.

The Valkyries described themselves as "being the Venomous Vaporings of Vituperative Vixens, Verses, and other odd matter, to get our minds off our stupid studies." Their slogan was "Vote for Vacations, Vacuity, Vim, Vigor, Valor, and Vampires." The Valkyries stated their purpose as "raising the standards of student life and in promoting deserving enterprises." The Valkyrie members were recognizable by the winged "V" emblem they wore proudly. Jessie Beghtol Lee assisted in organizing the Valkyries and suggested the winged "V" emblem. One of the founders of the Valkyries was Louise Pound, along with some of the progressive women students who had also been involved in establishing the WAA.

The Valkyries focused their attention on organizing the girls' football game day luncheons, female football rallies, women's athletics, female cheering sections at football games, the selection of female cheerleaders, and the female freshman convocation where they taught new female students school spirit through yells and songs. In fact, the Valkyries were responsible for selecting the 1919–1920 squad of female cheerleaders.

The origination of the name Valkyrie may have been a response to the men's junior honor society established in 1904 called the Vikings. Or possibly the name was derived from a fashionable German opera titled *Die Walküre (The Valkyrie)* by Richard Wagner, based on Norse mythology, and performed in Omaha in 1896. We may never know how the Valkyrie organization settled on its name, but the term "Valkyrie" is derived from Norse mythology referring to strong female figures in battle. Whether Norse mythology was the inspiration or not, it is a fitting name for those progressive women students.

Continuing the spirit in the female student cheer section, in 1922, in between halves of the football game, the females rolled down a red canopy with a large white "N" covering up the whole girls' section. A new tradition was started in the fall of 1922 when the female students were given red handkerchiefs and male students given white megaphones, and upon the cheerleaders' signal they waved these items for a scarlet and cream effect.

The University of Nebraska female students proved their enthusiasm for the game of football and, in combination with their organizations of the WAA, WSGA, the Valkyries, and the Black Masques, brought about equal opportunities in 1917, for the earliest known college females to cheer with men on the field. The male and female student cheering sections were now next to each other, and the need for cheerleaders to synchronize the cheering sections' yells became imperative to orchestrate an effective, unified cheering front at football games.

As women students were gaining strength on campus, beauty contests and beauty queens were becoming popular. Louise Pound made it known that she was against beauty contests judged solely on women's beauty and believed this was a setback to how far women had advanced. Pound expressed a strong opinion that women should be judged on their merit—for example, their intelligence or athletic ability. Not only did Pound believe this, she lived it as well. The members of the Valkyries shared in her opinion and in 1922 publicly condemned the idea of a beauty section in the *Cornhusker* yearbook. The female students wanted to be taken seriously.

The Daily Nebraskan reported the Valkyrie opinion on this matter:

> *This society (Valkyrie) knows of no woman among last year's contestants in the beauty section who really liked the situation in which she was placed. "We aren't Follies girls or actresses, and we do not expect to become moving-picture stars," said one of them, "and it gives us no particular pleasure to have the general public and the newspapers discuss the details of our features or our complexions or modes of hairdressing, or whether or not we are blondes or brunettes, or whether we aren't really homely, and got into the contest only through political friends." Many people of good taste and judgment, both in the city and on the campus, are against such contests, with their attendant attempts to foster inter-fraternity rivalry.*

The original opposition to beauty contests for female students by the Valkyries and Pound did not hold up. Starting in the 1930s, beauty queens and competitions were becoming even more popular for women on campuses, and a Nebraska Pep Queen was first elected from the Tassels in 1939. The selection of the homecoming queen and king remains today an annual event.

The University of Nebraska students were enterprising in creating organizations on campus, but in 1928, the Student Council determined there were too many organizations, and especially too many honor societies. Effective June 1, 1928, the Student Council abolished the Valkyries, along with the other organizations known as the Green Goblins, Mystic Fish, Iron Sphinx, XI Delta, Vikings, and Silver Serpents. The Innocents and Mortar Board survived the cut and remain on campus today.

The student cheering sections evolved into the Corn Cobs pep organization for male students, which was first organized in 1921. The idea to form an official male pep group evolved after the 1921 Oklahoma football game. Nebraska lost the football game 44 to 0, and what stood out at the game to the students and fans was the Oklahoma pep club's contribution to halftime and what they brought to the game. At the end of the half-time show, the Oklahoma Jazz Hounds pulled homing pigeons from their sweaters, and a mass swirl of birds was sent up into the sky. This act impressed the Nebraska students, and a decision was made for a Nebraska pep club to perform stunts at future football games. Their mission was to promote spirit and pep for all athletic activities.

Originally, membership was limited to two men from each fraternity and one from each college. Later, membership was comprised of men chosen by a ballot. By 1924 the Corn Cobs were self-supporting, generating funds from selling programs, "N" mum flowers, and the *Cornhusker* yearbook. They were also known for going on the field at home games during halftime and performing stunts.

The Corn Cobs sponsored pep rallies, arranging the card section, forming the spirit line, organizing homecoming, ushering at basketball games, arousing enthusiasm, managing the mascot, and encouraging interest in all athletics. By 1941, the Corn Cobs were very successful and considered one of the outstanding service organizations on the campus.

On February 23, 1924, the Tassels were founded under the guidance of the female senior honorary society, Mortar Board. The Tassels officially debuted at a football game as reported by the 1925 *Cornhusker* yearbook: "These young ladies put on their silk stockings and bloomers and paraded on horseback in front of the stands." The Tassels were now officially recognized as an organization on campus and worked side-by-side with the Corn Cobs to coordinate athletic activities and generate campus spirit. In staying with the corn theme with the pep organization names, the incoming freshmen were referred to as Kernels.

The Corn Cobs were actively involved with homecoming, for which the first homecoming displays were created in 1923. The displays had meager beginnings with expenditure limits of $25 in 1930, which increased to $300 in 1962 for combined displays and $200 for single displays.

A group photo of the 1922–1923 Corn Cobs all-male pep organization, which was formed in 1921 to boost spirit at football games.

First picture of the Tassels, the all-female pep organization during the 1924 school year. The Tassels worked in combination with the Corn Cobs to boost school spirit.

Homecoming 1943, with Yell King Jack Hogan escorting Pep Queen Polly Petty.

Card section at a game on September 30, 1950. The band on the field and the cards spell out "HI DAD."

Dealing with the Card Section

The first flash cards were created and displayed in 1925 by Oregon State University. Shortly thereafter, in 1927, the Innocents Society created Nebraska's card section, and the Corn Cobs and Tassels introduced the card section to the fans in the stadium.

Originally the Innocents named the card section the Husker Silent Cheering Section, and when introduced it was the only card section in the Big Six. Innocents member Carl Olsen was the first chairman of the section. The cards consisted of the colors of Nebraska and those of the opponents. The rooting section used the cards to make figures and letters of both teams.

By 1929, the card section made the University of Nebraska student rooting section one of the best cheering sections in the country. In 1930, it took 880 students to complete the section to carry out the flashing messages and images. The seats in the west stadium became the popular seats for fans so they could get a better view of the card section. In 1930, it was not uncommon to see cards flying in the air after a touchdown. The section's last image displayed during a game was always a white background with a large red "N." By 1951, the card section had swelled to 1,387 students. The displays consisted of the theme of the day and images to acknowledge visitors and the University.

The section stunts involved a total of five flashes, with the last two flashes not a set pattern. After the cards and directions were placed in the stadium seats prior to a game, the Corn Cobs stood guard so no one would change up the cards. The University card section was under student management, which was unlike other well-known university card sections, who hired a professional to create and run their sections.

At a game on September 30, 1952, the card section again threw their cards, which seemed to be a common practice over the years. At a game on October 5, 1970, the card section sparked controversy with fans and reprimand by band director Jack Sneider when the Corn Cobs devised a plan for a message that wasn't preapproved. The Vietnam War was in progress, and Nebraska played Army at home. General William Westmoreland was in attendance in the west stadium. The card section flashed "Love-Peace-Army" with a peace sign replacing the O in love—an apparent silent message of war protest to the general.

It happened again at a game on October 14, 1972, during halftime of a football game between Nebraska and Missouri. As usual, the morning of the game, the Corn Cobs placed cards in the stands; however, someone replaced the cards with new messages. The card-switching incident caused a major uproar on campus, and an investigation ensued, but at the time, the pranksters were never identified.

Years later, an article by Zach Pluhacek, a reporter with the *Lincoln Journal Star*, appeared on October 30, 2010, and revealed one of the pranksters involved in the card section change. An Omaha attorney, Sam Brower, confessed to the 1972 prank. A group of seven students called themselves "The Missouri Seven." According to Brower, to pull off the card trick, they had an insider involved—someone who was a member of the Corn Cobs and part of the group that was to oversee and guard the card section layout.

In the interview, Brower stated he was in charge of the Nebraska-Missouri Victory Bell for the Innocents, and he had easy access to the stadium on game day morning to bring in the bell for the game. The revised cards were assembled the night before. After placing the Victory Bell, Brower replaced the correct cards with the prank cards, located under each seat in the card section.

The revised prank messages flashed "Devaney for President," "Johnny R. is shifty," [referring to Heisman Trophy winner Johnny Rodgers] and the last message, "Screw Mizzou." All messages were displayed in the card section. According to Brower, he and his cohorts-in-crime were never caught and punished, but the newspaper interview now seemed like the time to confess, due to guilt he felt over the years.

During an incident on a rainy, windy game day on October 22, 1977, at the Colorado game, cards were tossed in excitement of the game and flew in the stadium and injured several fans. The cards were lost and ruined. In the past, when cards became lost or ruined, the practice was to charge the card section members a fine. After this particular game, the members were fined for the ruined cards, and the fees were collected by the band's director. But the band director did not replace the cards, which led to the demise of the card section.

The card section had a prime spot in the east stadium, and the band director was motivated to oust the card section, so the band could take over the choice seats. He even went as far as to announce at a February Gamma Lambda (the band's honorary fraternity) meeting that the band would be moving to the middle section, formerly held by the card section. This change did not come to fruition for the band because the University made the decision to reserve the prime seats to sell to season ticket holders. The student card section ended at University games during the 1977 season.

In recent years, the card section was temporarily resurrected on two occasions. The first was to honor our country and the victims of the September 11, 2001, terrorist attacks on the United States. Due to the tragedy, the football game between Nebraska and Rice was postponed that weekend and played on September 20, 2001 (a Thursday). Although this was a solemn occasion, the University made the football game a heartwarming day. To honor the victims, the players approached the field through the Tunnel Walk in silence. The card section flashed "U.S.A." in red, white, and blue. The resurrection of the card section served to bring back tradition and salute special events.

A second resurrection of the card section occurred for Tom Osborne's last game, as he retired as the University's athletic director. The east stadium fans flashed red and white cards with messages of "Thanks Tom" and "Go Big Red" at a game on Saturday, November 17, 2012, prior to the start of the game. In the past, the students led and operated the card section, but for current card tributes, a professional company, Kivett Productions, arranges the cards, and the flashes are performed by fans.

Fan card section at a game on November 17, 2012, honored former coach and athletic director Tom Osborne as he retired from the University of Nebraska.

War, Student Unrest, and the Boneyard

In 1944, the Corn Cobs had disbanded temporarily due to World War II, so the Tassels took the lead in continuing the pep club duties. After the war, the Corn Cobs and Tassels once again worked together to promote spirit and enthusiasm on campus in support of athletic events for many years. However, in the 1960s and 1970s during times of student attitude changes, campus unrest, and antiestablishment feelings, organizations began to lose favor and student interest. As the student attitude on campus shifted, many organizations suffered or disappeared. But the Corn Cobs and Tassels were able to carry on as organizations.

In 1977, the organizations began to feel the effects of Title IX. With equality on the minds of some of the female Tassels members, they expressed an interest in wanting to join the Corn Cobs organization and were open to having the Corn Cob members join the Tassels group. There were discussions of combining the two organizations and renaming the group, but this idea did not materialize. By 1980, male and female members were intermixed within the two organizations. Shortly thereafter, the two organizations no longer existed, along with other pep organizations around the country.

In recent years, the University of Nebraska student section in Memorial Stadium has become known as the Boneyard. The name is a symbol of the Blackshirts and identified with "throwing the bones." The Blackshirts originated around 1964 as a way for Coach Bob Devaney to easily identify his defensive players during practice.

The student section known as the Boneyard at the UCLA game, September 14, 2013.

The story goes like this: Assistant Coach Mike Corgan was sent out to pick up a different color practice jersey and accidentally started a beloved tradition. The sporting goods store the assistant coach visited had a large lot of black jerseys that hadn't sold, so they made a good deal on the jerseys. The wearing of the black jerseys started as a daily practice jersey and evolved into a reward for the top defensive starters. It wasn't until a September 7, 1985, football game against opponent Florida State that the symbol of the Blackshirts was first revealed on a banner in the end zone.

The intimidating design of the skull-and-crossbones was created by Husker fan, graphic designer, and print shop owner Tim Riley. Riley's print shop, Gnu Graphics in Omaha, had a mouse problem. To help solve the problem, he purchased several boxes of mouse poison, which displayed a poison warning. According to Brandon Vogel of *Hail Varsity Magazine*, "The international sign for poison is a skull-and-crossbones, a symbol conveying danger since it was used on pirate flags during the 18th century." The conveyance of danger seemed a perfect symbol for Nebraska's defensive front. The poison symbol on the box inspired Riley with the idea to symbolize the Blackshirts.

Once Coach Tom Osborne approved the use of the design to symbolize the Blackshirts, the look became identifiable and popular with the Cornhusker fans. The first player to cross their arms in an "X" to symbolize the bones after a play on the field was a walk-on linebacker, Matt Hunting, in 1996. The whole defensive team picked up on "throwing the bones," and the rest is history and a treasured tradition.

Pep Rallies and Bonfires

A rousing speech, the band playing the school fight song, the cheerleaders leading the students in chants, marching and carrying lit torches, and snake dancing from campus through the streets of Lincoln are all highlights of pep rallies in the early years of University of Nebraska athletics.

The professors considered it very important for students to support the football team prior to the games with rallies and a spirited send-off at the train station for away games. It was also just as important to wait and celebrate their return, win or lose.

A November 11, 1910, article in *The Daily Nebraskan* reported, "Members of the team say it was the Nebraska enthusiasm displayed at the Kansas rally and the send-off given them the night of their departure for Lawrence that won the Jayhawker's game. No doubt this is true, for the enthusiasm displayed and the exhibition of school spirit among the students was enough to inspire the football players on to mighty deeds of valor."

When football began on campus and through the first half of the twentieth century, pep rallies were highly popular. Rallies always varied in some degree, but usually consisted of motivating speeches by the chancellor, coach, professors, and players. The attendance at pep rallies would range from hundreds to thousands of students cheering, chanting, and singing school songs, along with music provided by the band.

The cheerleaders would be in attendance to generate enthusiasm. Torchlight parades going back to the 1930s were common with the band, cheerleaders, and students walking through downtown Lincoln and on the University campus. Sometimes the parades and rallies were followed by a bonfire on campus.

One such pep rally in 1902 featuring a parade and bonfire had 1,000 to 1,500 students in attendance. After parading through town, the students scattered to collect wood for a bonfire. An article in *The Daily Nebraskan* dated October 20, 1902, recounts the activities: "Several wagons were filled with boxes, barrels, and crates and pulled at a run through the streets on their way to the gridiron where the fire was to be built." The wood was stacked approximately twenty-five feet in the air. The students joined hands around the fire, shouting and dancing. Also reported in the article, "The band boys, who had occupied a position in the grand stand, were placed in a delivery wagon and hauled around the field playing 'Hot Time,' and other lively tunes."

The Corn Cobs and Tassels pep organizations worked with the cheerleaders to plan rallies and parades. In 1942, a rally committee was created that consisted of

Students gather at a 1959 pregame pep rally.

Traditional bonfire and pep rally on the eve of homecoming 1959 before the Missouri game.

Bonfire and pep rally, 1960–1961 season.

a representative from the Innocents Society, Student Council, Tassels, and Corn Cobs to take charge of the planning.

During the late 1970s, any remaining social unrest on campus generated by opposition to the Vietnam War was starting to slowly dissipate. A renewal of school spirit was beginning to be felt on campus. Bonfires had become a thing of the past, and pep rallies and parades had been reduced to only a few prior to the big games. The rallies now consisted of the cheerleaders parading with the band and ending at a location downtown or on campus. The head coach would give a speech, along with the football captains. The cheerleaders would perform routines to school songs and lead cheers of "Go Big Red."

Soon a trend was beginning to emerge of holding additional rallies exclusively by the cheerleaders off campus in which they performed cheers and dance routines to generate fan enthusiasm. The pep rallies have evolved into several pregame appearances starting four hours prior to the kickoff of a home football game.

Cheerleaders promote school spirit at a traditional pep rally in front of a large gathering of students in 1959.

Pep rally parade through the streets in 1967.

First pep rally of the fall football season 1977, at a downtown location. Pictured are Herbie Husker, the Yell Squad, and Coach Tom Osborne speaking to the crowd.

In the late 1970s, a tradition was started on Friday nights before home games to perform at Misty's Restaurant in Havelock (a suburb of Lincoln). The current Spirit Squad still carries on this tradition at Misty's. On game day, the current squad also performs and generates enthusiasm at the Embassy Suites Hotel in downtown Lincoln, as well as at various locations and events around town. The squad performs at the University of Nebraska President's and Chancellor's events, the Pavilion, Champion Club, and various tailgate parties.

Whether it is the old style or the new style of pep rallies, the purpose is still the same—to generate fan enthusiasm and excitement leading up to the football game. And who had the loudest "voice" on campus during games? The band, of course.

9

Pride of the Cornhusker State — The Band

"There they are, the pride of the Cornhusker state, the University of Nebraska Cornhusker Marching Band!" This announcement blares out on game days as the band takes the field in Memorial Stadium.

The "Band Song" is sung by the band members as they march on parade and prior to playing the "Hail Varsity" school song. The lyrics of the "Band Song" were written by band members while riding a train to the Rose Bowl in the 1940s.

"Band Song"

Hear the Trumpets playin'
Hear the crowd a sayin'
NU Band is on parade!
Hear the Trombones blowin'
Hear the Drums a rollin'
NU Band is on parade!

Sound Out! Sound Out!
Sound out loud and clear
Let the team all know

> The Band is here
> Sons of old Nebraska
> If someone should ask ya
> We're the Scarlet and the Cream!

The three hundred and one members of the Cornhusker Marching Band outfitted in scarlet and cream shine as the sun glints off their brass and silver instruments. In and among the band, sparkle is added by the flag corps waving their flags in unison and the twirlers catching sky-high baton throws.

The elaborate routines and number of band members in today's Cornhusker Marching Band is a drastic contrast to the band's humble beginnings. The band started as an ROTC corps of military cadets working on their drilling and marching. The teaching of military science was a requirement for establishing a land-grant university according to the Morrill Land Grant College Act of 1862, under which the University of Nebraska was founded. Military drill by the students was on a volunteer basis until 1877, when drill became mandatory for all students due to waning interest in the military.

The University of Nebraska Cornhusker Marching Band started as a military band. This is the earliest known picture of them taken in Omaha at a drill competition on July 3, 1881.

The Cornhusker Marching Band first performed a formation at a 1926 football half-time show. This "N" formation was performed at a game on September 15, 1937.

Lt. Isaac T. Webster arrived at the University in 1879 and would later become known as the father of the Cornhusker Band. His goal, according to band member Gary Steffens, was to "put some spirit into the otherwise drab routine of military drill." When Webster arrived, he realized the only marching music the cadets were provided was by a lone piccolo player. It became Webster's mission to provide music to increase interest in the military, and thus, a military band was formed.

The first Cornhusker Band was formed in 1879 and the student director in charge was Percival Everitt. The band was a twelve-piece ensemble, and Everitt was the only member who could play an instrument.

Roscoe Pound was a member of the military cadets and became the band's drum major in the 1880s. Drumming up pep, excitement, and enthusiasm, the band played at baseball games prior to the arrival of football on campus. Once football was organized, it was natural and fitting for the band to play at football games. The band created school spirit with pep and song and also entertained the fans in attendance.

In 1901, the band performed their first half-time show, which quickly became a regular event. During the Nebraska vs. Missouri game in Lincoln in 1926, the band performed their first formation—the letter "N" on the field.

The first time the "Star-Spangled Banner" was played at the start of a game in Lincoln was in 1926. By 1928, the Cornhusker Marching Band was one of the largest university bands in the country. The popularity of the band continued to grow, and, as a result, membership grew to 104 students during this time. A problem developed when administrators realized there were only ninety band uniforms available. Band graduates were contacted and asked to return their uniforms so the whole band could be outfitted.

Marching to the Beat of Big Bertha

The generic name given to the familiar big bass drum used by college marching bands is Big Bertha. The name is derived from the famous German Big Bertha Howitzer cannon. The University of Nebraska has had its own Big Bertha since 1931. But first, some history of these big boomers.

The first big drum was constructed in 1921 when the Leedy Manufacturing Company was contacted by Purdue University band director Spotts Emick. The cost of the drum was $911.12. Purdue says their drum still stands approximately 10 feet tall, but they keep the exact measurements a secret. Yet it is said to be a similar size to the University of Texas drum.

The Purdue drum made its first appearance in a football game against the University of Chicago. After the game, the University of Chicago band contacted Conn Instruments and requested a bigger drum. In 1922, the University of Chicago had their big drum when they played Princeton University. Their large drum was 8 feet in diameter, 44 inches deep, and when measured from the base of its wheeled cart to the top of the drum, it stood 10 feet tall and weighed over 500 pounds.

The large drum was later retired at the University of Chicago when the school ended their varsity football program in 1939. The drum was abandoned under the bleachers of the stadium and left to deteriorate until 1955. At that time the University of Texas Longhorn band director rescued the old drum, purchasing it for $1. The University of Chicago was probably happy to sell the drum, since it was determined the drum was radioactive. The radioactivity occurred because

The Cornhusker Marching Band during a half-time performance with the Big Bertha drum.

the Chicago stadium was turned into a bomb testing site called the Manhattan Project to develop a nuclear bomb for World War II. As a result, the drum sitting under the bleachers was affected.

When purchased by the University of Texas, the drum was restored and has been used during games during the band's pregame and half-time shows, and after touchdowns at all home games. The University of Texas and Purdue University have had an ongoing controversy, both claiming to have the largest Big Bertha drum.

These large drums are rare and were not mass produced, so there are very few of them used today. The University of Missouri is home to a big drum named Big Mo.

The University of Nebraska has had a Big Bertha drum since 1931, when it was purchased by John Selleck, the business manager at the time for the athletic department. The drum was never officially named, but was generally referred to as Big Bertha, and the University's drum stands at 7 feet tall. The making of the large drums was tricky, and it took special cow hides that were large enough to cover the frame and were supplied by the Omaha stockyards. At the time the drum was unveiled at Nebraska, it was only one of three big drums in the country.

The drum was retired and put in storage after the 1941 Rose Bowl game, but was brought back into service in September 1961 and used until the mid-1970s for special games including homecoming. Once again, the drum was retired and it currently resides with the Alumni Association for safekeeping.

WOMEN JOIN THE RANKS

World War II took a toll on the band, as it did with other organizations. Because men were away fighting for their country, a positive change resulted due to the war during the fall of 1942. For the first time, women were allowed in the Cornhusker Marching Band to fill the gaps left by the male students away in combat. Not only did the band suffer from the war, but the football team and the cheerleading squad did too. The war opened the door for female cheerleaders to reappear on the field during the fall of 1944, and for female students to take the lead in organizations on campus.

The University of Nebraska Band has been winning awards over the years, and in August 2013, the University released this statement: "The Marching Red has received many honors throughout its 134-year history, including a Distinguished Recognition Trophy presented by John Philip Sousa in 1927 and the John Philip Sousa Foundation's Sudler Trophy in 1996 for high musical standards and innovative marching routines. The Sudler Trophy is the highest honor given to collegiate bands."

The band has received national attention since college football became a regular feature on prime-time television starting in the 1950s. The band has made appearances on television programs, such as NBC's prime-time series *Tommy*

The band's Big Bertha drum at the Champions Club prior to a football game in October 2014.

Lee Goes to College in 2005, ABC's *Extreme Home Makeover: Home Edition*, and then again in the motion picture *Yes Man* starring Jim Carrey in 2008.

Another first for the University of Nebraska Marching Band was when they performed at the Rose, Orange, Fiesta, Sugar, and Cotton Bowls, making them the first collegiate band to perform at all the major football bowl games.

The University of Nebraska Band was organized and ready to participate from the beginning of Nebraska football, to lend support and spirit to the game day experience, and aid in the team's victories. Drum roll, please.

The Cornhusker Marching Band is led onto the football field by the drum major, October 27, 2012.

10

THE RAZZLE-DAZZLE OF THE POMPON SQUADS AND THE SCARLETS DANCE TEAM

WITH PRECISION HIGH KICKS, FLARE, AND GLITTERY POMPONS, THE UNIVERSITY of Nebraska dance team, drill team, pompon squad, and dance squad perform choreographed routines at sporting events to the delight of fans.

The first drill teams in the United States were started in 1929 by two Texas women. Gussie Nell Davis taught physical education in Greenville, Texas, and was asked to take over sponsorship of the high school pep club. She coordinated dance moves set to music and called the squad the Flaming Flashes. At the same time, Kay Teer at Edinburg High School in Texas formed a dance group with fifty girls who had not made the cheer squad. They were called the Red and Blue Sergeanettes and performed on the field during a 1936 football game halftime.

Davis was eventually offered a position at Kilgore College, where she created the Kilgore Rangerettes. In 1939, the Rangerettes were the first college drill team established and are still considered one of the best college drill teams. They are famous for their performances around the globe.

The first attempt at organizing a pompon squad that was separate from the cheerleaders at the University of Nebraska was in the fall of 1960. The Huskerettes, a group of sixteen women with pompons, were added to the band. The Huskerettes had recently been formed just prior to Jack Snider taking over as the band director. According to band member Gary Steffens, Snider had this to say about the Huskerettes:

> *A group of our fans had seen a performance by the Kilgore Rangerettes, and we got a lot of agitation to have a similar group march with the band. These people had no idea how such a group was organized or what relation it would have with a band, but they thought if Texas could have them there was no reason Nebraska couldn't also have them. They managed to get support from the administration and we were simply told that we would have to organize a group like them. Cost was no object, so we auditioned a bunch of girls and costumed them, and we got Mrs. Peg Maly from the Physical Education Department to help train them. I was never really sold on them. They never really sold the way they might have. The costumes were not very scanty and had they been more revealing, it might have been different.... After the second year, we were going to have to replace eight or ten of the girls, so we were going to need that many new costumes. When the administration heard that, they decided they didn't want to finance it anymore. They dropped it just as quickly as they insisted we have them in the first place.*

Most of the women on the Huskerette pompon squad did not have marching band experience. They never quite gelled with the band or connected to the fans, so at the end of the season, the Huskerettes were discontinued.

The 1963 football season brought a new look on the sidelines. A new pompon squad was formed under the direction of the University's first cheerleading coach, Jake Geier. The squad was an immediate success. The cheerleaders had used the same uniform style since the 1930s, but the new pompon squad brought change and excitement with a classic new uniform. They performed pompon routines and dances that had never been seen before on the Nebraska sidelines.

The pompon squad added a new element of spirit and enthusiasm to football and basketball games since they were the first squad to perform routines to school songs, as well as dances to other pep band songs.

The pompon squad was popular with the fans because they showcased a style fitting and representative of the University of Nebraska. This led to a unification of the cheerleaders and pompon squad into one unit starting in the fall of 1964.

First pompon squad wearing red-and-white-striped sweaters. (From left) Jean Barber, Susie Keating, Sandy Stefanisin, Georgia Merriam, Sandy Lane, Carolyn Daubert, Becky Haas, 1963–1964.

The pompon squad was the first to perform dance routines to school songs at football games starting in 1963.

Huskerettes performing at halftime with the band at the Kansas State game on October 20, 1962.

The pompon squad's style was adopted, including their uniforms, dance routines, and cheers. Combined, they were known as the Yell Squad.

Over the next several years, the University was without a separate dance squad. In the spring of 1979, a female student formed a new dance squad, also named the Huskerettes. The head basketball coach at the time was Joe Cipriano, and the basketball organization was approached with the idea of having the new dance squad perform at basketball games during halftime. Coach Cipriano was in favor of the idea; he knew it would bring excitement, entertainment, and fan involvement to the basketball games.

A new genre of popular music in the 1970s was disco, so the dance squad brought recorded disco music and performed fast-paced, contemporary routines for fan half-time entertainment. The squad wore glittery red dress uniforms and white knee-high boots. The spirited performances were new, different, and exciting, and the students and fans enjoyed the flashy show. However, the Huskerettes were never a University-sanctioned organization, and without full support of the athletic department, the group disbanded a few years later.

THE SCARLETS DEBUT

The Scarlets—the first dance team, 1992.

After the end of the Huskerettes, the athletic department was approached at times by students with the desire to form another dance squad. No one had brought the athletic department a complete and feasible plan of action for a new group until 1991. A student named Krismichelle McPherson devised and presented a complete and acceptable plan to the athletic department for a dance team named the Scarlets.

The Scarlets were an immediate hit and received an enthusiastic response from the crowd. They proved themselves with their dazzling choreography, talent, style, grace, and flare, and became an asset to game day. The first squad of Scarlets were Tracy Thompson, Cheryl Peterson, Michelle Matthies, Jenny Horner, Nikki Jackson, Tricia Eldien, Martha Dunn, Halle Beverage, Jenny Chopp, Liz Beffa, Kristen Hogensen, Karen Cartensen, Amy Franzen, Molly Keenan, and founder Krismichelle McPherson.

By way of background, in the fall of 1991 incoming freshmen at the University of Nebraska were not allowed to be members of the Yell Squad and there was no dance team. Krismichelle McPherson, a native Lincolnite, took it upon herself to start one. The Scarlets are now an integral part of the Spirit Squad and a fixture at athletic events. I have taken this history from a recent personal communication with her.

Dance teams contribute to the overall game atmosphere and entertain the crowd. While there is some overlap in their function with cheerleaders, the two squads require different skill sets.

Then a student, McPherson sought a faculty sponsor and approached academic advisor Carol Grell, who was supportive of the idea of providing students with an opportunity to enhance their academic pursuits at the University and graciously agreed to be the faculty sponsor. McPherson was the first person to call the dance team the Scarlets. From there the question was whether it would be a student organization or part of the athletic department.

She met with the administration at the athletic department armed with a proposal for introducing a dance team. The proposal included a code of conduct for members, audition criteria, uniform suggestions, and a budget. At that time, it was communicated that there had been other students who had tried to get a dance team started, but the athletic department did not feel that those groups were prepared to handle the responsibility of being under the athletic department and lacked organization.

For the first time, the athletic department saw potential for a dance team. The athletic department felt they could not commit taking on a dance team. However, if McPherson could put together a team, she was told they would provide the team with performance opportunities at men's and women's basketball games. It was also discussed that if the team did well, there was the potential to be incorporated into the athletic department in the future.

With student signatures and an application process completed, the group was given permission to proceed with their plan for creating a dance team by the Association of Students at the University of Nebraska. This organization is the student government at the University and oversees student involvement on campus. The dance team created formal bylaws for operation as well.

The first audition date was set in spring 1992. Informational meetings were held, an advertisement appeared in *The Daily Nebraskan*, and radio advertisements bombarded the KFRX radio waves. A choreographer donated time to create tryout routines, judges were secured, and local dance studios provided staff to teach the routines. Operating on a zero dollar budget proved to be complicated, according to McPherson.

"On the day of tryouts, no one knew what to expect. Over 350 brave women showed up at the Recreation Center to audition for the dance team. They learned a short dance and performed different dance skills as part of their audition," McPherson said.

At the end of the day, approximately forty women were asked to come back for finals. Finals took place the next day at the Military and Naval Science building. At the end of that day, seventeen women became the first Scarlets.

The Scarlets attended National Dance Alliance (NDA) Collegiate Dance Camp in summer 1992 on campus. At that time, there was an NCA/NDA college camp that was held in Lincoln. The cheerleaders were present at camp and supported the new dance team. The two programs operated separately that first year. Team members paid for camp themselves; in fact, that first year, the entire program was fully funded by the members.

Dance practices began in the fall of 1992 at 6:30 a.m. each school day at the Recreation Center. "It was difficult to find practice space as the team was not part of the athletic department or the dance department, had no budget, and was not known to the campus community," McPherson said.

The Scarlets' debut performance took place at a pep rally on Halloween weekend 1992 at the Coliseum. The group was met with loud cheers and great enthusiasm from the attendees. Their next performance took place that same weekend at Midnight Madness, a men's basketball scrimmage game.

That first year, the Scarlets performed at most men's basketball games and several women's basketball game halftimes. In later years, the team would dance at timeouts during games. The Scarlets became adept at creating dance numbers where dancers faced fans in all corners of the Bob Devaney Sports Center so no fans felt left out. Some routines included props, and even once incorporated pulling a prank on the audience while dancing to the song "Oklahoma!" at the Oklahoma vs. Nebraska game. Herbie Husker played along with the prank and the crowd went wild!

McPherson convinced the athletic department to let the team perform at the football pregame in 1992. This was an important opportunity for the athletic department to see the value that a dance team could provide to football games. Knowing that they had a lot to prove, the team worked diligently to prove their dance ability, showmanship, and how they could get the crowd involved and excited. To the credit of the team, the athletic department was impressed. So much so that they invited the Scarlets to become part of the athletic department starting in 1993.

Those first Scarlets paved the way for future Scarlets to receive athletic scholarships, to dance at national championship games, to travel to games and tournaments, as well as national dance team competitions. Cheerleaders and dance teams each have their own nationals. The first time the Scarlets competed nationally was at the 1994 NDA Collegiate Nationals. They placed sixth overall with a routine choreographed by team members themselves.

The Scarlets have gone on to compete and place as high as second at nationals. At the time of the publishing of this book, the Scarlets have gotten away from competing nationally in order to focus on game day. However, should the budget allow for it in the future, their hope is to return to competing.

Since the beginning, the Scarlets have entertained and thrilled the Cornhusker fans with their award-winning style and performances. The Scarlets were the perfect addition to the Yell Squad and mascots to create a well-rounded Spirit Squad and complete the whole game day experience for the fans.

II

From Bugeaters to Cornhuskers and Corn Cob Man to Herbie Husker — The Lore Behind the Team Names and Mascots

You may have heard of the Bugeaters—an earlier name for the Nebraska team—but you may not be so familiar with the Treeplanters, Rattlesnake Boys, or Antelopes. These names were tied to and used to describe Nebraska teams in the late 1800s.

When two football teams came together on the field, it was important to have established school colors to set the universities apart from each other. The development and spread of intercollegiate football created a need for college identity and to show the students' loyalty to the school. One way to foster loyalty was to create a nickname for the football team, which eventually evolved into naming a mascot.

The first college mascot appeared in 1879 at Princeton. The inspiration for creating the Princeton Tiger was the orange and black stripes on the Princeton football players' socks. Mascot nicknames also evolved for further team identification. In 1889, the first nickname of a mascot was Handsome Dan, the Yale bulldog.

Mascots have become a natural part of athletics, campus life, and school pride. This was demonstrated at the University of Nebraska in 1995, when there were rumors of Herbie Husker's demise after the athletic department considered replacing him. Herbie is so beloved in the Cornhusker State that the fans and students rallied to save Herbie. The students considered Herbie a tradition and a representative of school spirit, so he was saved and his character lives on.

According to Kris Burns and Traci Weinstein, authors of a book about mascots, "Mascots are described as a person, animal, or object that is believed to bring luck to those who worship it." Often, mascots are represented by real animals or people costumed with large head pieces. It takes skill for a person to transform their personality into a mascot, and it is considered by many to be an art form.

In addition, according to the authors, "The key to becoming a mascot is 'character.' Character is the sum of a mascot's personality, because once in costume, it is merely not enough to act a character, but one must become them. The person in costume no longer exists as an individual, but as their character. Of all the components of character, personality is perhaps the most crucial. The character of a mascot is reflected through the personality, both behaviorally and physically."

A mascot has the power to generate crowd enthusiasm, and it is important for a mascot to be positive and to connect with the fans. According to Roy Yarbrough in his book, *Mascots: The History of Senior/Junior College and University Mascots and Nicknames*, "A mascot is an identity, a source of entertainment, a rallying point. Each college or university desires to represent their school in a unique way forever hoping that 'their' mascot will bring them victory."

The University of Nebraska was first known as the Old Gold Knights, a name selected for the team by Roscoe Pound. When the colors changed from old gold to scarlet and cream, their nickname also needed to change. Newspaper reporters would use descriptive monikers to describe the team, pulling from words that described the state of Nebraska. Some of these early names included Treeplanters, Rattlesnake Boys, Antelopes, and Bugeaters.

The most commonly used of these early nicknames was Bugeaters. Though we may never know exactly how the name Bugeaters came to be, there are a couple of theories. In the 1870s, a journalist came to Nebraska to write a story on the drought conditions and reported the bugs were eating the corn, leaving nothing for the people to eat except the bugs. There are also birds in Nebraska called nighthawks which are nicknamed bugeaters, and they fly around eating all the bugs. The pioneers of Nebraska endured hardships on the Great Plains frontier, surviving droughts and grasshopper invasions. The name Bugeaters may have been a positive term to describe the hardiness of the Nebraska pioneers to do what it took to survive the harsh conditions and may not have literally meant eating bugs.

Early image of Johnny Husker from the 1950s.

It was common for a school's mascot to change and evolve through the years as universities formed their identities. The University of Nebraska went through several nicknames before they settled on the name Cornhusker. It was Charles "Cy" Sherman, a sports editor, who named the team the Cornhuskers in 1899. He didn't feel the earlier names were appropriate. Charles Sherman was later called the Father of the Cornhuskers.

The football team of 1900 was the first to use the Cornhusker name. Thus, by the turn of the century, the University of Nebraska was known as the Cornhuskers and was loyal to the colors of scarlet and cream. In the late 1930s, the Nebraska Legislature further cemented this name by naming Nebraska the "Cornhusker State." In recent years, the name Cornhusker has been shortened, the team often being referred to as the Huskers. New 2018 head football coach Scott Frost has stated he prefers tradition and uses the name Cornhusker.

So what does a Cornhusker look like? This became a question the University would struggle with through the years as the Cornhusker mascot evolved. By the 1950s mascots were a major part of college football. A first attempt for Nebraska to have a mascot happened when the Yell Squad brought a young Jersey calf on the field for a few of the football games in the fall of 1955. However, that same season, Corn Cob Man made his first appearance at a home game against Colorado. The Corn Cobs, the male student spirit organization, were involved in creating Nebraska's first mascot and paid for the mascot's head. The Corn Cobs were in charge of the mascot until it became a member of the Spirit Squad in the late 1980s.

In the early years, the student wearing the mascot costume did not try out for the position; the Corn Cobs would merely assign someone for each game to fill the mascot outfit. In the 1960s, a sophomore student named Harvey Perlman (later to become chancellor) filled in one game as Corn Cob Man for a fraternity brother who couldn't make the game. Perlman's one and only time as the Corn Cob Man took place in Boulder at the Colorado game.

According to Yell King Gene Christensen, the Corn Cob Man mascot head was fashioned after the University of Kansas Jayhawk mascot. To create the first mascot head, Christensen contacted a Minnesota company. *The Daily Nebraskan* reported, "The head was hand-made by the same woman who made the bear used in connection with the 'Land of Sky Blue Waters' commercials of a malt beverage company."

In teaming with the Corn Cobs on the project, the Tassels were in charge of ordering the outfit to be made so that Corn Cob Man would have a complete outfit to wear with his head piece. The mascot's debut featured only the head since the outfit was still being constructed. The full mascot outfit was featured during the following home game when Nebraska played Oklahoma.

Corn Cob Man with a member of the Tassels.

The Corn Cobs pep organization chose a new mascot and named him Huskie the Husker in 1962.

Mr. Big Red or Harry Husker was created by Bill Goggins and was used as an unofficial mascot from 1970 to 1973. This image was used through 1988 for promotional purposes.

The Corn Cob Man's look featured a head piece resembling a half ear of corn with green fabric leaves on top, and a painted, simplistic face. To complete the outfit, the uniform consisted of green coveralls. The mascot was basically an ear of corn, and it was not reflective of the desire to convey a strong, dominant team image for the Cornhuskers.

Encouraged by the athletic department, in 1962 the Corn Cobs created a new mascot that was considered to be more representative of a Nebraskan. The new mascot wore a plaid shirt, bib overalls, and a bucket-style straw hat sitting atop his papier-mâché head. The new mascot stood ten feet tall and was named Huskie the Husker.

In the spring of 1965, the spirit committee of the Student Council was looking for a new spirit symbol or mascot to replace Huskie the Husker. The council reviewed three choices: Husky Herf the Bull, Bob the Cob, and The Big Tough Guy (who showed a similar look to the brand mascot Mr. Clean). Husky Herf won the approval of the council and the support of *The Daily Nebraskan*.

When presented to the athletic department, they opposed the Husky Herf spirit symbol, therefore ending its consideration. In the late 1960s, Nebraska still did not have an official mascot. The Cornhusker fans have always been passionate one way or another about the team's mascot, chiming in with suggestions of a miniature of the State Capitol or possibly live animals such as a red bird, a fox, or an Irish Setter dog.

In 1970, a drawing caught the attention of Ticket Manager Jim Pittenger and Sports Information Director Don Bryant. It was a cartoon in an issue of *Nebraska Farmer* magazine of a Husker fan who was dressed in a red blazer, and a cowboy hat, waving an "N" flag. They obtained permission from artist Bill Goggins and the magazine to reproduce the cartoon for use by the athletic department.

Known by two names, Mr. Big Red or Harry Husker, the mascot attends a football game in 1970.

Debra Kleve White, author of this book and then a cheerleader for the wrestling team, shows her affection for Herbie Husker, 1976.

Mascot head of Mr. Big Red or Harry Husker, 2018.

The red mini fire engine was driven on the field to celebrate touchdowns in the 1970s.

Pregame Tunnel Walk with Lil' Red, Ohio State game on October 14, 2017.

The newly designed Herbie Husker was unveiled in 1974.

Herbie Husker debuting with a refurbished face, 1986.

They named the cartoon Mr. Big Red and wanted to move in the direction of using it on stationery and calendars. Mr. Big Red was also referred to by the name Harry Husker and Mr. Cornhusker. According to a report written by Schlievert and Rosowski, "Responsibility for naming him Harry Husker lies with the *Omaha World-Herald* because the newspaper used him to predict football scores in a weekly feature entitled 'Harry's Predictions.'"

A fiberglass mascot head was constructed to represent Harry Husker, and a student wore it to complete the outfit. He'd then walk the sidelines and mingle with fans. The head weighed approximately 70 pounds, looming 5 feet 8 inches tall, and was balanced on top of a student's shoulders. The head had its problems—it was heavy, hot, and hard to control on windy days. Because of these issues, the contraption could only be worn forty-five minutes at a time, requiring students to switch off the wearing the mascot head.

Herbie Husker with another modification to his face, 1988.

Yet another update for a more buff Herbie Husker, 2003.

According to Schlievert and Rosowski, "The design was modeled after members of the Hastings Chamber of Commerce who wore red blazers and big cowboy hats to the football games." He was a natural fit at the time because Nebraska fans' popular game day attire was a red felt cowboy hat with a white "N" displayed on the front, just like the one Mr. Big Red sported.

The Corn Cobs took care of Mr. Big Red, deciding who would wear the mascot head and transporting it to games. The mascot head was so large that it could not fit in the cargo space of a bus when the team traveled; therefore, the Mr. Big Red head had to travel separately in its own van.

Even though Mr. Big Red was used for promotion and walked the sidelines at football games, he was never adopted as an official University mascot.

As Tom Osborne was taking over as head coach in 1973, Husker fans would witness a red, miniature fire engine driven onto the field to celebrate a scoring touchdown. The fire truck which sported two sirens, a loud speaker, and played the school fight song, and was driven by members of the Corn Cobs. Husker fans also considered the fire truck as somewhat of a mascot.

Pace Woods, the owner of Woods Brothers Realty, had seen a similar fire truck at a San Francisco 49ers football game and thought it would make a good addition to game day at Nebraska. He presented the idea to the athletic department, and they approved it. Woods ordered the new Nebraska fire truck and donated it to the Corn Cobs and Tassels pep organizations for spirit use on home game days.

As a mascot, Mr. Big Red walked the sidelines until 1974 when a new symbol caught the eye of Sports Information Director Don Bryant. He had spotted a cartoon on the wall of the Cotton Bowl media headquarters of a Nebraska fan in overalls with an ear of corn in his back pocket and a football in his hand. It was beside a cartoon of Bevo, the Texas Longhorn. Artist Dirk West of Lubbock, Texas, was contacted for permission and was asked to paint a new, more refined and complimentary cartoon.

The athletic department commissioned West to provide the new painting—now on display at the Bob Devaney Sports Center—and it was copyrighted and reproduced on the cover of the media guide to introduce the first official Nebraska logo. Don Bryant is considered the Father of Herbie Husker, since he discovered and named him.

After the debut of the Herbie cartoon drawing in 1974, a bib-overall–costumed Herbie Husker mascot was unveiled by the Corn Cobs, walking the sidelines at football games. The new Herbie Husker mascot head was designed by Bob Johnson, a former Disney Studios artist, for the cost of $1,500. The University sent Johnson a picture of John Dutton, a former Nebraska football player who played the seasons of 1971–1973. Dutton was also a former pro player for the Baltimore Colts and Dallas Cowboys. A caricature in Dutton's likeness was used as the basis for the new look of the Herbie Husker head.

The Herbie Husker mascot head was much anticipated, but sparked some disappointment by Husker fans when it debuted. Some felt he was too similar to Oklahoma State's Pistol Pete. This was not a surprise, since Johnson had also designed Pistol Pete's head, and the two mascots shared similar characteristics.

An opinion piece sent to the editor of *The Daily Nebraskan* by a Nebraska fan, Mary Voboril, panned the new Herbie: "The shaggy-haired, vacant-eyed, wrinkle-faced Mad Hatter is representative of Big Red—no thanks." Continuing the controversy, the *Lincoln Journal Star* held a mascot poll: "The results… 9% of the respondents liked the new mascot and 21% preferred the old mascot. Seventy percent said they disliked both."

During this time, Mr. Big Red (Harry Husker) remained a promotional mascot and symbol with the athletic department and was utilized in conjunction with Herbie Husker. During the mid-to-late 1970s through 1988, the mascots were interchangeably called Herbie and Harry (yes, confusing). Mr. Big Red (Harry Husker) was managed by the Corn Cobs, and Herbie Husker was managed by the Yell Squad. However, in 1988 the University discontinued the use of Harry Husker, and Herbie Husker became the only mascot, still part of the Yell Squad team. The name "Herbie" proved to be most popular and won out as the official mascot name.

In 1982, Herbie was once again redesigned with a fuzzy face and buggy eyes. Throughout the 1980s and 1990s, every few years a worn-out Herbie costume was sent off to mascot manufacturers for a new costume and facelift. The reactions were not always favorable. In 1987, for example, the Greek yearbook stated, "Herbie Husker's new mask was a topic of controversy across campus." Also criticized was the $4,000 redesign in 1996, with comments of "yikes" and "Herbie's new look just plain scary." After his debut appearance at a game, an editorial in *The Daily Nebraskan* called the new Herbie "an ugly stereotype of Nebraskans in general and an unfavorable symbol of the Cornhuskers in specific."

The *Journal Star* reported similar reactions in 1995 during Bill Byrne's sidelining of Herbie: "Some fans supported Byrne's decision, saying the farmer-in-overalls mascot perpetuated an image of Nebraska as a hick state. At one point the athletic department temporarily agreed, when Bill Byrne sidelined Herbie in 1995. Others kicked off a passionate protest to keep the mascot." The supportive fans of Herbie Husker won out and Herbie remained as a member of the Spirit Squad.

In 1993, a change was made to have an additional mascot on the field or court with Herbie Husker, and Lil' Red—a young male mascot—was introduced. Lil' Red was created by an Omaha-based company called Signs and Shapes International, Inc. The idea for Lil' Red was brought about by Associate Athletic Director Dr. Barbara Hibner, who was a supporter and champion of the betterment of the athletic department and sports opportunities for female student athletes. According to Huskers.com, "Hibner is a supporter of the progress and advancement of women's athletics at Nebraska and throughout the nation. In the past nine years, soccer (1994), bowling (1997), and rifle (1998) have been added, making Nebraska the Big 12 leader with thirteen sports programs providing women 117 scholarship opportunities."

The need for that second mascot appeared in 1992 when the University of Nebraska had three sporting events in one day—football, basketball, and volleyball. Herbie was needed at all three events, but because of time conflicts, he could only make two of the three. The volleyball game lost out on the mascot appearance. This led to the creation of another mascot. The new mascot's name came from a contest arranged by the University of Nebraska athletic department's marketing team for the students of Lincoln elementary schools.

At times, the mascot duties were supposed to be split among events, but the two mascots were always intended to work together. Having two mascots at one school is special, since few universities can claim to have two outstanding mascots to represent the school.

Lil' Red was a new phenomenon for Cornhusker fans. He was a trendsetter, being one of the first inflatable mascots created for sporting events and a first of his kind as a mascot.

Lil' Red is a large, inflated balloon character with a youthful look, wearing his hat sideways. Lil' Red has a variety of tricks and antics that he performs on the field. He entertains the crowd with many maneuvers, including spinning around, running, dancing, and jumping up and down on his head. Lil' Red has been described as a puffy WalkAround® mascot and looms large at 8 feet 4 inches, but is also lightweight. The student operating the costume wears a belt with an air circulation system that keeps the mascot inflated. He was originally introduced with the young fans in mind, but Lil' Red is universally enjoyed by fans of all ages and continues to be a fan favorite.

ESPN college football commentator Kirk Herbstreit said Lil' Red is his favorite mascot and noted, "Lil' Red is a crowd favorite, and his trick of bouncing on his head is welcomed by all spectators at sporting events."

Over the years, the look of the mascots continues to evolve to stay updated, relevant, and representative of the University. The current look of Herbie Husker is taller, bigger, and more muscular. He was revealed in the fall of 2003, when Herbie came onto the field riding in a golf cart shaped like a football helmet. Leading up to the launch of Herbie's new look, information was released that the University had put Herbie on a diet and a strict workout regimen to get in shape.

The change in Herbie came about as a result of the University wanting an updated look to better represent the agricultural Cornhusker State and represent an image of Nebraska showing strength and power. The 2003 redesign accomplished these goals, and Herbie's new look has since been embraced as an endearing symbol of Nebraska.

All of the mascots at Nebraska have consisted of a student wearing a large head piece with another student wearing a costume (except the inflatable Lil' Red), and as the new head pieces replaced the old head pieces, the old ones mysteriously disappeared from the University. The mascot heads can be found anywhere from local businesses to being stored in a fan's basement. The head of Mr. Big Red (Harry Husker), used from 1970 to 1988, was found abandoned in a storage unit in Lincoln. The new lessee of the storage unit owned a local downtown bar, and Mr. Big Red (Harry Husker) was on display in the bar for many years until the bar was sold. On February 13, 2016, Mr. Big Red's (Harry Husker) mascot head was sold at auction to the highest bidder.

A national Mascot Hall of Fame was established in 2005 by David Raymond and is located in Newark, Delaware. Each year mascots are elected into the Mascot

Hall of Fame by a voting membership and executive committee. The mascots go through a nomination process and are placed on a ballot for consideration. A public online vote contributes to the final decision. "The mission of the Mascot Hall of Fame is to honor mascot performers, performances, and programs that have positively affected their communities," according to the group.

Lil' Red's work as a mascot in 1999 won him the title of national Mascot of the Year. In 2005, the Herbie Husker mascot received the same award. Herbie's award was celebrated during halftime of the 2006 Capital One Bowl. In 2007, Lil' Red was inducted into the Mascot Hall of Fame. The popularity of Lil' Red continues today as shown by the NCAA ranking Lil' Red in January 2016 as the number-one inflatable mascot in the country.

The names of Cornhusker mascots have included Corn Cob Man, Huskie the Husker, Mr. Big Red, Herbie Husker, Harry Husker, and Lil' Red. Currently the University of Nebraska's two official mascots are Herbie Husker and Lil' Red. According to Huskers.com, "Nebraska's mascots are two of the most popular figures around the community, as well as the state, and the pair usually generate quite a bit of energy wherever they appear."

There is no doubt that the award-winning performance, style, and personalities of the University of Nebraska mascots bring enjoyment to the Nebraska fans and are a positive addition to game day, both on and off the field.

A Final Hurrah

The spirit of Nebraska was envisioned and formed by early Nebraskans, led by the Pounds, and nurtured by the Spirit Squad throughout the years, bringing this spirit forward to how we recognize it today. The goals set in 1903 and by all Spirit Squad members past and present have created and modeled a respect for the opponents, a sense of fair play, knowledge of the game, and an undying support for the team, which has established and carries on the true spirit of Nebraska.

The University of Nebraska's Spirit Squad has provided tradition, entertainment, and enthusiasm, and has successfully brought together and led the student body and Cornhusker fans through innovation, creativity, and style. A statement written in the 1909 *Cornhusker* yearbook is as relevant today as when it was written.

> *College spirit is just as essential for the advancement of a university as patriotism is for the advancement of a nation.*
>
> *College spirit differs widely in different localities according to the manhood and womanhood of the student body: it may be good or bad—one of fair play, or of narrowness. Therefore, it is necessary in the growth of our "Nebraska Spirit," symbolized by the "Scarlet and Cream," that we look to the highest ideals and establish standards that will reflect the glory of our great state. Let us develop such a spirit in the undergraduate and alumnus that the fellowship of college chums and classmates at Nebraska will be cherished in the after years and create an undying love for Nebraska and our Alma Mater.*

Let us further promote the spirit of cleanness and fair play whether upon the athletic field or in intellectual pursuit that our opponents may be filled with admiration for our practicum, and respect for the institution which we represent.

Both Yale and Harvard are known for the quality of their spirit, which is now firmly established and reflected in their college traditions. May the "Nebraska Spirit" grow.

There is not a "last" chapter to this book. As with anything of importance, the hope is that the University of Nebraska Spirit Squad will live on. It is inevitable it will change and grow. However, the only certainty with school spirit and cheerleading is change. Change has been a part of the Spirit Squad in the past, and change will happen in the future, to ensure enthusiasm and evolution of the squad. It must evolve as it has in the past, to perform at the highest level possible.

We must remember there is value in preserving and celebrating our tradition and history, yet understand that there is value in evolving. Both are important to serve and support the University, athletic events, the student body, and the Cornhusker fans. May the spirit of Nebraska continue to grow.

Notes, Sources, and Bibliography

Readers are referred to the website www.SpiritofNebraska.com where there is compiled a lengthy list of notes, a bibliography, and sources used in compiling this history of the University of Nebraska.

ACKNOWLEDGMENTS

A PROJECT OF THIS NATURE AND MAGNITUDE IS IMPOSSIBLE WITHOUT collaboration, support, and generosity of time. Contributing time, interest, and cooperation were the University of Nebraska, the University Athletic Department, the University Alumni Office, *The Daily Nebraskan*, the past and current Spirit Squad members, past and current Spirit Squad coaches, the Nebraska State Historical Society, and the University of Nebraska Love Library's Archives and Special Collections, and the librarians who became my friends.

I was honored when Dr. Tom Osborne agreed to contribute an inspirational foreword for this book. Your moving and heartfelt contribution fulfilled and exceeded my wildest dreams, and your support and written words meant more to me than you will ever know.

I was inspired by former cheerleaders in their interviews providing personal stories, historical accounts, and memories. I found a special connection to Anna "Hink" Aasen Sahs, John "Jack" Hogan, Marge Arendt Wilnes, Ike Walter, Ralph "Whitie" Reed, Art Pickerton, and Harry "Kam" Kammerlohr. I admire their kindness and energy, and I am proud to call them my friends.

The Cornhusker connection can bring together the common bonds of strangers, and this is true of Dr. Jim Cox, University of Texas at Austin, whom I thank for your interest and assistance in this project. Also, thank you for the introduction to Robert "Bob" Jones, PhD candidate at the University of Texas at Austin. A tremendous amount of appreciation to Bob for agreeing to participate and edit, due to our common interest in sports. Your talent in crafting the English language and guiding me to help make this book special is an amazing gift. Thanks for sharing your gift with me.

A tremendous amount of appreciation to Dr. William Nethercut, professor at the University of Texas at Austin, for his time and generosity in translating Roscoe Pound's Latin songs. It was a pleasure working with you.

My dear friend and Yell Squad sister Sally Lorenzen, thank you for your time in reading and talent in editing. Your support, insight, and contributions were invaluable. I can always count on Sally's witty sense of humor to provide laughter and to light up my spirit. During this process, Sally was my personal cheerleader, encouraging me and keeping me motivated.

A special thank you to Suzan Karrer Rohrig who voluntarily and selflessly referred me to Concierge Marketing and Book Publishing Services in Omaha, Nebraska, to look over my project. I don't know where this project would be today if it weren't for your referral.

A special thank you to the incomparable Lisa Pelto and her staff at Concierge Marketing, for understanding the project and bringing it all together. This book would not have become a reality without their talented guidance. Also, Lisa knew the perfect editor to partner with me, and I feel fortunate and grateful to have worked with Sandra Wendel.

I am especially thankful for the expertise provided in the Innocents chapter of the book by Ryan Wilkins, Amanda Hergert Brown, and the 2014–2015 members of the Innocents Society. Your special insight is particularly important considering the secrecy of the society. Thank you all for taking the time to read the chapters and confirm their accuracy.

A heartfelt thank you to Krismichelle McPherson Zolcik for contributing her knowledge and input on the Scarlets dance team. Krismichelle is a visionary and responsible for creating the Scarlets in 1992, and through her perseverance and guidance, the Scarlets became a reality and an official team of the Spirit Squad in 1993. The world needs more people like Krismichelle to roll up their sleeves to get a job done, and at the same time doing it fabulously.

Readers are helpful in providing their opinions from an outside point of view. Thank you to my readers Greg White, Keri White, and Nathan White. To my sweet friend Jeanne Tanous, who has a heart of gold, thank you for taking the time to read cover to cover and sharing valuable writing insight and giving much needed constructive suggestions. To my longtime, dear friend Mary Stone, your enthusiasm and interest in reading the book and especially the chapter about Louise Pound spoke to my heart.

Thank you Ross and Julie Jernstrom for your enthusiasm, support, and believing in this project and me. When there was doubt, you gave me encouragement.

Thank you Joshua Caster, Love Libraries Archive and Special Collections Department, for your knowledge, willingness to help, and tireless research on my behalf.

Two special authors inspired me during my journey: Marie Krohn, author of *Louise Pound: The 19th Century Iconoclast Who Forever Changed America's Views about Women, Academics, and Sports*. During the writing process, the chapter I struggled with the most was on Louise Pound, because it was difficult to do her justice in the confinement of a single chapter. It was important to me to properly convey how everything about Louise was special, how she was a one-of-a-kind human being born before her time. Marie Krohn captured her amazing essence. Thank you, Marie, for reading the chapter about Louise; it meant a lot to me to get your blessing on such an important chapter.

Kathy Nelson, author of *More Than Football: George Flippin's Stromsburg Years*. The generosity of Marie and Kathy to meet with me to discuss Louise Pound, George Flippin, and their books was selfless, inspiring, and moved and motivated me. In times of trials and tribulations, I could hear Kathy's voice in my head, "If I can do it, you can do it."

Five special Spirit Squad coaches have touched my life. Thank you to Dr. Bill "Murph" Murphy for being my coach, mentor, and father figure for three years in college and the years beyond. "Thank you" simply isn't enough for selecting me, allowing me to be a part of an amazing tradition with a great group of people. Everyone deserves to know they have made a positive contribution in the world and made someone proud. Thank you for being my someone. You will never know the impact you have had on my life. You are special and adored.

Dr. Kris Baack, professor, former Spirit Squad coach, and mentor. Kris's guidance, professionalism, leadership, and most importantly, friendship, was invaluable during the 2003 reunion and "100 Years of Cheer" celebration. Also during the 2003 reunion, former Yell Squad member and coach, Renee Black, provided selfless assistance with her career connections and event knowledge. In the reunion planning, Renee became a friend whom I came to discover as truly beautiful inside and out.

Starting in 1950, the first Yell Squad coach was Jake Geier. I would like to thank Jake for agreeing to an interview. It was an honor to meet him, and through him I could clearly visualize how the glory days of the Yell Squad developed. I was moved by his intensity, clarity, generosity, and dedication to perfection. Finally, the current Spirit Squad coach Erynn Nicholson Butzke, thank you for all the meetings, information, and support. I see the passion, dedication, and care you bring to the Spirit Squad. You are amazing. There are only a small, select group that have been chosen and privileged to lead the Spirit Squad at the University of Nebraska and to truly know the dedication, sacrifice, and reward that comes with the job. I am proud to know you all.

From one Yell Squad member to another, I want to thank Nancy "Jonesy" Jones. Thank you for noticing me, believing in me, and validating me as a person and a future Yell Squad member. Jonesy, you changed my life, directed it down the right path toward passion and purpose, and I will be forever grateful. Most important, Jonesy, thank you for allowing me to walk in your shoes.

Louise Pound was a great woman who lived an extraordinary life. I admire Louise for her trailblazing attitude, her story which inspired me and I believe has made me a stronger woman. I wish all young girls could know her powerful magic and magnificence and the strength she brought to being female. Kristi Lowenthal, in her thesis, stated this about Louise Pound: "Her favorite former students created an informal alliance called the 'Louise Pound Alumni Association,' and Pound once said that the group's 'devotion and loyalty' meant more to her than all her academic achievements and accolades. 'I believe the pleasantest thing that has happened to me,' she told a reporter on her retirement, 'is that I've had a number of books dedicated to me.'" It is my hope this book pleases you, too, Louise.

To my Yell Squad family of friends, with whom I had the amazing pleasure to cheer with during my three years on the squad. Looking back on my life, I can honestly say my Yell Squad sisters and brothers are some of the best people I have ever had the pleasure of knowing. Your friendship, support, laughs, acceptance, and unconditional love forever transformed, inspired, and moved me: Julie Hurt Johnson, Karen Kirwan Weiner, Griff Davenport, Tim Holscher, Chris Lofgreen, Julie O'Meara Jernstrom, Sally Pearson Lorenzen, Sandy Perkins Aletraris, Shelley Reissener Thompson, John Slavens, Susan White, Patti Charvat, Liz Held Stromath, Lee Chapin, Scot Cockson, Russ Hoffbauer, Cindy Jones Dumas, Deneé Nelson, and Kim Welsh Hise. To all of you, since the day we met, we have had a special connection and shared experience that has placed each one of you forever in my thoughts and most of all in my heart. I feel privileged and honored to have shared our college years and years beyond, and that our lives will be forever connected through the Yell Squad spirit—and the human spirit.

About the Author

Debra Kleve White is a native Nebraskan. As a graduate of the University of Nebraska (UNL) and a former Yell Squad member (1977–1980), her education and college experiences led her toward a path of gratitude and a desire to give back to the University. In doing so, she developed her passion for history and research, concentrating on the UNL athletic department and Spirit Squad, where her love lies.

Her belief in education led her to the University of Texas at Austin, where she works in the College of Education, Institute for Public School Initiatives. She is also a real estate broker in Austin, Texas.

The Spirit of Nebraska is her first book. Deb currently lives in Austin, Texas, but the distance does not deter her from returning to Memorial Stadium in the fall. She may not be wearing the cherished red-and-white wool sweater or saddle shoes, or waving pompons on the sidelines, but her voice is just as loud as it was on the field with the Yell Squad cheering on her beloved Cornhuskers.

(On left) Debra Kleve White today. (On right) UNL Yell Squad, 1977–1978. Debra is pictured on the bottom row on the right.

Photo Credits

To request more information about a specific photo,
please use the archive photo number provided.

Archive Photo #   **Photo Credit** .... **Page, Location**

COVER

89	UNL Athletic Department and UNL Photo Services	front cover, top
166	Ross Jernstrom	front cover, bottom
17	Archives & Special Collections, University of Nebraska-Lincoln Libraries	back cover

INTERIOR

181	University of Minnesota Archives	16
182	University of Minnesota Archives	17
60	Archives & Special Collections, University of Nebraska-Lincoln Libraries	19, left
63	Archives & Special Collections, University of Nebraska-Lincoln Libraries	19, right
64	Archives & Special Collections, University of Nebraska-Lincoln Libraries	22
65	Archives & Special Collections, University of Nebraska-Lincoln Libraries	23
66	Archives & Special Collections, University of Nebraska-Lincoln Libraries	25, top left
67	Archives & Special Collections, University of Nebraska-Lincoln Libraries	25, top center
68	Archives & Special Collections, University of Nebraska-Lincoln Libraries	25, top right
69	Archives & Special Collections, University of Nebraska-Lincoln Libraries	25, middle
70	Archives & Special Collections, University of Nebraska-Lincoln Libraries	25, bottom
71	Grainger family	26, top left
72	Grainger family	26, top right
73	Grainger family	26, bottom

75	Harry Kammerlohr	27
74	Archives & Special Collections, University of Nebraska-Lincoln Libraries	28, top left
117	Archives & Special Collections, University of Nebraska-Lincoln Libraries	28, top right
77	Ike Walter	28, bottom
79	Archives & Special Collections, University of Nebraska-Lincoln Libraries	30
80	Edholm-Deputron & Blomgren Commercial Photographers – Blomgren Family	31, left
78	Archives & Special Collections, University of Nebraska-Lincoln Libraries	31, right
111	Archives & Special Collections, University of Nebraska-Lincoln Libraries	33
82	Archives & Special Collections, University of Nebraska-Lincoln Libraries	35
83	Archives & Special Collections, University of Nebraska-Lincoln Libraries	36
110	Archives & Special Collections, University of Nebraska-Lincoln Libraries	37
85	UNL Athletic Department and UNL Photo Services	39
87	Archives & Special Collections, University of Nebraska-Lincoln Libraries	41, top
90	Sharon Finney and Geri Finney Moore	41, bottom left
95	Debra Kleve White Collection	41, bottom right
98	Chris Raff and Chuck Hoffman	42
97	Chris Raff and Chuck Hoffman	43
99	Chris Raff and Chuck Hoffman	44, top
129	Debra Kleve White Collection	44, middle
128	Rance Ristau Photography	44, bottom
171	*Lincoln Journal Star* - Randy Hampton	45
1	Archives & Special Collections, University of Nebraska-Lincoln Libraries	52
2	Jim Fields Collection	57
3	Archives & Special Collections, University of Nebraska-Lincoln Libraries	59
4	Jim Fields Collection	63
59	Jim Fields Collection	64
5	UNL Athletic Department and UNL Photo Services	66
137	Debra Kleve White Collection	70
7	Nebraska State Historical Society	78
8	Nebraska State Historical Society	82, left
104	Archives & Special Collections, University of Nebraska-Lincoln Libraries	82, right
9	Nebraska State Historical Society	86
76	Ed Dosek	94
11	Nebraska State Historical Society	95
12	UNL Innocents Society	97
105	Debra Kleve White Collection	100
62	No credit, printed 1901, public domain (New Yells)	113
32	UNL Alumni Association	123

30	Lyrics credit: Wilbur Chenowith and W. Joyce Ayres	124
31	Lyrics credit: Harry Pecha and UNL Alumni Association	127
170	Debra Kleve White Collection, *Nebraska Songs*, UNL Alumni Association 1922	129
106	Archives & Special Collections, University of Nebraska-Lincoln Libraries	130
180	Debra Kleve White Collection	131

(CREDITS FOR INTERIOR CONTINUED ON PAGE 210)

PHOTO ALBUM

mem3	Debra Kleve White Collection	A, top left
mem6	Debra Kleve White Collection	A, top right
mem1	Debra Kleve White Collection	A, bottom
132	Mitch Otto Photography	B, top
124	Rance Ristau Photography	B, bottom
133	Mitch Otto Photography	C, top
134	John Clabaugh	C, bottom left
131	Mitch Otto Photography	C, bottom right
91	Joe Mixan Photography and Geri Finney Moore	D, top left
130	Sheila Iburg Hosher and Crystal Zabka Belsky	D, top right
121	Rance Ristau Photography	D, bottom
92	Chris Raff and Catherine Foster Krauter	E, top
57	Robin Netz and Mallory Netz	E, middle right
97	Chris Raff and Chuck Hoffman	E, bottom left
113	Mitch Otto Photography and Jennifer Powell	E, bottom right
99	Chris Raff and Chuck Hoffman	F, top
166	Ross Jernstrom	F, bottom
98	Chris Raff and Chuck Hoffman	G, top left
167	Scott Bruhn/UNL Photo Services	G, top right
139	Stanton Shirk and Sara Shirk	G, bottom
142	UNL Athletic Department and UNL Photo Services	H, top left
143	UNL Athletic Department and UNL Photo Services	H, top right
165	UNL Athletic Department and UNL Photo Services	H, middle right
145	UNL Athletic Department and UNL Photo Services	H, bottom left
146	UNL Athletic Department and UNL Photo Services	H, bottom center
147	UNL Athletic Department and UNL Photo Services	H, bottom right
148	UNL Athletic Department and UNL Photo Services	I, top left
149	UNL Athletic Department and UNL Photo Services	I, top center
150	UNL Athletic Department and UNL Photo Services	I, top right
151	UNL Athletic Department and UNL Photo Services	I, middle left

152	UNL Athletic Department and UNL Photo Services	I, bottom left
153	UNL Athletic Department and UNL Photo Services	I, bottom right
154	UNL Athletic Department and UNL Photo Services	J, top left
155	UNL Athletic Department and UNL Photo Services	J, top center
156	UNL Athletic Department and UNL Photo Services	J, top right
158	UNL Athletic Department and UNL Photo Services	J, middle right
157	UNL Athletic Department and UNL Photo Services	J, bottom left
159	UNL Athletic Department and UNL Photo Services	J, bottom right
160	UNL Athletic Department and UNL Photo Services	K, top left
161	UNL Athletic Department and UNL Photo Services	K, top right
162	UNL Athletic Department and UNL Photo Services	K, middle left
163	UNL Athletic Department and UNL Photo Services	K, bottom left
164	UNL Athletic Department and UNL Photo Services	K, bottom center
136	UNL Athletic Department and UNL Photo Services	K, bottom right
125	Rance Ristau Photography	L, top
96	UNL Athletic Department and UNL Photo Services and Lisa Belden with LB Photography and Courtney Belden	L, bottom
55	National Cheerleading Association (NCA) and Tamara Johnson Serafini	M, top left
123	Rance Ristau Photography	M, top right
122	Rance Ristau Photography	M, bottom
118	Rance Ristau Photography and Jennifer Powell	N, top left
101	Kivett Productions	N, top right
119	Rance Ristau Photography	N, bottom
144	UNL Athletic Department and UNL Photo Services	O, top left
56	UNL Athletic Department and UNL Photo Services and Krismichelle McPherson Zolcik	O, top right
58	Sherene Al-Turk	O, middle right
126	Rance Ristau Photography	O, bottom
140	Bob Olson "The Picture Man" Photography and Judy Olson	P, top
135	John Clabaugh	P, bottom left
127	Rance Ristau Photography	P, bottom right

INTERIOR CONTINUED

108	*The Daily Nebraskan*, Nov. 7, 1902	151
24	Archives & Special Collections, University of Nebraska-Lincoln Libraries	153
18	Archives & Special Collections, University of Nebraska-Lincoln Libraries	158, top
19	Archives & Special Collections, University of Nebraska-Lincoln Libraries	158, bottom
22	Archives & Special Collections, University of Nebraska-Lincoln Libraries	159, top
21	Archives & Special Collections, University of Nebraska-Lincoln Libraries	159, bottom

100	Kivett Productions	162
123	Rance Ristau Photography	163
116	Archives & Special Collections, University of Nebraska-Lincoln Libraries	165, top
25	Archives & Special Collections, University of Nebraska-Lincoln Libraries	165, bottom left
26	Archives & Special Collections, University of Nebraska-Lincoln Libraries	165, bottom right
115	Archives & Special Collections, University of Nebraska-Lincoln Libraries	166
114	Archives & Special Collections, University of Nebraska-Lincoln Libraries	167, top
27	Alan Hilt	167, bottom
13	Archives & Special Collections, University of Nebraska-Lincoln Libraries	170
15	Archives & Special Collections, University of Nebraska-Lincoln Libraries	171
17	Archives & Special Collections, University of Nebraska-Lincoln Libraries	173
103	Debra Kleve White Collection	174
120	Rance Ristau Photography	175
88	UNL Athletic Department and UNL Photo Services and Sandra Stefanisin Berris	179, top
53	UNL Athletic Department and UNL Photo Services	179, bottom left
89	UNL Athletic Department and UNL Photo Services	179, bottom right
54	Anderson Studios Photography and Molly Keenan Ebaldi	180
33	UNL Athletic Department	187
36	UNL Athletic Department and UNL Photo Services	188, top left
37	UNL Athletic Department and UNL Photo Services	188, top right
39	UNL Athletic Department and UNL Photo Services	188, bottom
40	Archives & Special Collections, University of Nebraska-Lincoln Libraries	189
43	UNL Athletic Department and UNL Photo Services	190, top left
138	Debra Kleve White Collection	190, top right
109	UNL Athletic Department and UNL Photo Services	190, bottom left
51	Debra Kleve White Collection	190, bottom right
42	UNL Athletic Department and UNL Photo Services	191, left
44	UNL Athletic Department and UNL Photo Services	191, right
45	UNL Athletic Department and UNL Photo Services	192, left
50	UNL Athletic Department and UNL Photo Services	192, right
AP	Author Photo Courtesy of: Cori Greener Roberts Photography	205, left
1977	UNL Athletic Department and UNL Photo Services	205, right

www.ingramcontent.com/pod-product-compliance
Lightning Source LLC
Chambersburg PA
CBHW050459110426
42742CB00018B/3309